Inspirational Stories of How Angels
Weave the Tapestries of Our Lives

Angel Threads

Bob Danzig

Danzig Insight Services, Inc.

Angel Threads

Published by Danzig Insight Services:
www.bobdanzig.com

ISBN: 978-0-9855129-8-9

Book and Cover Design by Kira Rosner:
www.KiraRosner.com

Printed and Distributed by Lightning Source Inc.
www.LightningSource.com

Special note of gratitude to the remarkable artistic design of the talented Vicki Heil and Josh Klenert and the inspiring tapestry rendering –unique in the universe – from the heart and hands of Michelle Piano, whose combined gifts created the interior, cover design, and cover art for the first edition of this book.

Thanks is given to *Ladies' Home Journal* for allowing us to reprint a portion of the 1997 article Heavenly Creature (Copyright 1997, Meredith Corporation. All rights reserved. Used with permission of *Ladies' Home Journal*.)

Dedication

To all those unique threads who have enriched my personal tapestry. Each and every one of them has been an angel to me, especially my five children.

Acknowledgements

Every book starts as a raw idea which may remain just that until talented folk come your way and cause you to add flesh to the idea. The so rich talents who nurtured the idea of *Angel Threads* to reality include Rabbi Susan Werke, Sherry Weintraub, always my precious children, the gifted Callie Rucker Oettinger, and book designer, Kira Rosner. Each added unique dimension as the book moved from embryo to maturity. My gratitude to all is deep and permanent.

Table of Contents

Contents

Contents

"Heavenly messengers walk among us."

Foreword
by Mrs. Og (Bette) Mandino

The upright stone marker for the grave of my gifted life partner, husband Og Mandino, stands tall with a shining granite face deeply engraved with the full front picture of an angel. Not just any angel, but the delicate engraving of a seraphim that satisfied Og's unique requirement that the angels he collected must have feet. "Those angel feet," Og would say, "show a heavenly messenger anchored by feet to walk the Earth among us."

Og, as affirmed by the boxcars of fan mail for his books and speeches, was a messenger of hope and possibility for the tens of millions who found guidance, direction and reasons to embrace tomorrow in his words. Many would describe him as their "angel" sent to engrave his message upon their spirit.

My Og was an anchored man. The valleys of his life only caused him to place his own feet more firmly as he climbed the mountains of success as a husband, father, grandfather, author, speaker and friend. Yes, Og was deeply engraved in the minds and hearts of those he touched.

And now, you, my dear reader, can be engraved in the life tapestry of others as you choose to be an angel thread. Your own life can be enhanced as you are open to the angel threads offered for your tapestry. As you meditate on the stories Bob Danzig has collected in this remarkable book, *Angel Threads*, please do see the spirit of my dear Og hoping your life is deeply engraved.

With much love,
Bette Mandino

"Mystical threads weave our tapestries."

Introduction

Her hand reached past me as she placed her items next to mine at the checkout counter. But her being premature in placing down all her goods was not what made me turn around. It was the pin she was wearing. Out of the corner of my eye, I could see the gold guardian angel snuggled on her white sweater just above her heart. And again, I was amazed at the overwhelming presence of angels in society. It made me wonder where I had been living that I had failed to notice the popularity of angels and how I had missed out until now on something so wonderful.

It was in the sixth class of a series of classes I was taking to learn more about the Jewish faith when I first began to understand the impact of angels on society. Having been placed in foster care at the age of two, the home I was put in, and the four following it, recognized the interpreted religion of my mother. Therefore, I was raised Catholic, with no linkage or even basic understanding of my Jewish birth father's heritage, traditions, or faith.

So when the Jewish Community Center near my home offered a course on Jewish life rhythms, it seemed to me a uniquely rich opportunity to develop an appreciation of that half of my heritage. And, in the sixth class, when the energetic, young, woman rabbi instructing had my class focus on the presence of angels in the Jewish faith, I began to feel myself focusing in on a generations-old influence I had never previously considered.

On the Saturday following that class, Sherry Weintraub, wife of my good friend, Steve Weintraub, joined our morning walk/bagels group for the first time ever. During our chat she asked about the subjects being discussed in my Jewish life rhythms class, and I filled her in on the most recent focus on angels.

As Sherry listened with truly rapt attention, tears slowly began to flow down her cheeks. She dabbed with a tissue and then told us she was moved because the issue of angels is so central to her life. Sherry told us of attending a party some years back when the hostess had engaged a fortune teller as the entertainment. Because she had to leave the party early to attend another function, Sherry was urged by the hostess to be the first one to visit the fortune teller. Resisting, she explained to us, "because she always felt such metaphysical ideas were bunk," she only agreed to sit to satisfy the hostess.

Looking into her eyes, the fortune teller said that Sherry had an angel protecting and guiding her. Sherry responded with a disparaging laugh. When the fortune teller said the angel is a male, Sherry laughed again at such nonsense. And when the fortune teller said it is a boy named Irving, Sherry withdrew from the specific suggestion, declaring that she had no boy named Irving in her life—ever. She was urged, she said, to close her eyes and reflect before she rejected this information. Sherry did so and suddenly a clear picture of her departed father, whom she loved dearly, appeared in her mind. She could hear his voice reminding her of the fact that he had a nine-year-old brother who had died at that very young age. His name, the image of her dad said, was Irving. When Sherry left the party, she walked away knowing much more than she had arrived with. She left with the comforting knowledge that she had been permanently blessed with the presence of Irving. Her tears over coffee were simply an acknowledgement of the special blessing her angel presence had in her life. "To me," she said, "Irving is a thread of life in my personal tapestry."

Around the same time Sherry shared her story with me, I was retiring as the senior corporate executive of the Hearst Newspaper Group and vice president of the Hearst Corporation, and was starting my second career as a public speaker. Having been the product of the kindness that various key individuals bestowed on me over the years, I spent the time in most of my speaking engagements talking about the tapestry of life developed thread-by-thread by the various experiences and individuals we meet. The thrust of my talks was not to show how I found success in my family and business life, but to show how great is the ability we have to influence each other.

In many ways, Sherry's wonderful acknowledgement reaffirmed my belief that by sharing my reflections on the blessings in the tapestry of my life, a tapestry woven by all the vibrant and beautiful threads given to me by the individuals I have met and the experiences each opened, I could open others to their unique ability to affect happiness in themselves and, more importantly, in others. In doing this, I began to reflect on the specific qualities of the individuals who had strengthened my tapestry, and in so doing, discovered the defining term encompassing these qualities to be angel.

Through *Angel Threads*, my purpose is to help you see the special qualities in the threads that have shaped your tapestry and encourage you to be open to these threads, permitting them to weave their beauty into your every day.

–Bob Danzig

Setting the Structure

YOUR ANGEL

Barefoot and dirty, the girl simply sat and watched the people go by. She never tried to speak and never said a word. Many people passed, but not once did anyone stop. It just so happened that the next day I decided to go back to the park, curious to see if the little girl would still be there. Right in the very spot where she was the day before, she sat perched on high with the saddest look in her eyes.

I finally decided to walk over to the little girl. As we all know, a park full of strange people is not a place for young children to play alone. As I began walking toward her, I could see that the back of the little girl's dress indicated a deformity. I assumed that was the reason why people merely passed by and made no effort to help. As I moved closer, the little girl lowered her eyes to avoid my intent stare. I could see the shape of her back more clearly. It was grotesquely shaped in a humped over form. I smiled to let her know it was okay. I was there to help, to talk.

I sat down beside her and opened with a simple "Hello." The little girl acted shocked and stammered "Hi" after a long stare into my eyes. I smiled and she shyly smiled back. We talked 'till darkness fell and the park was empty.

When I asked the girl why she was so sad, she simply looked at me with a soulful face and said, "Because I'm different."

I immediately said, "That you are!" and smiled. "You remind me of an angel, sweet and innocent." She looked at me and smiled. Slowly she stood and said "Really?"

"Yes ma'am. You are like a little guardian angel sent to watch over all these people walking by."

She nodded her head yes and smiled, and with that she spread her wings and responded, "I am. I'm your guardian angel," with a twinkle in her eye.

I was speechless and sure that I was seeing things as she said, "For once you thought of someone other than yourself. My job here is done."

I immediately got to my feet and asked, "Why did no one stop to help an angel?"

She looked at me and smiled, "You are the only one who could see me, and you believe in your heart." And then she was gone. With that, my life was changed dramatically. So, when you think you are all you have, remember, your angel is always watching over you.

—Anonymous

*"The idea that nothing is true except
what we comprehend is silly."*
—WINSTON CHURCHILL

WHEN I FIRST STARTED my research into angels, I began asking family and friends if they had ever had an experience with an angel. Maybe they were all humoring me, as friends and family are known to do, but when I explained the reason for my research—to find a connection between the influences of angels and our everyday life, they were all enthusiastic and encouraging. Some even began sharing stories such as Sherry had. This response prompted me to extend an invitation to other friends and colleagues, and just about everyone else I met along the way, to share their stories—their "angel threads" with me.

Although everyone I asked seemed to have an idea as to what angels are, their ideas proved to vary quite a bit, as did their willingness to share them. For whatever reason, I found most people to be more comfortable discussing their experiences with strokes of life, random out-of-the-ordinary coincidences and moments of pure inspiration—such as a composer hearing his life's masterpiece playing in his head for the first time. But when it came to Divine Intervention and experiences with angels, the numbers dropped.

Why is this? Is it because influences by angels seem most acceptable for martyrs and saints? Or, is it because those who have had these experiences haven't recognized them as such?

Although not everyone can acknowledge an encounter with an angel, one thing is certain—everyone seems to have an opinion, be it a strong belief or a lingering doubt.

SOON AFTER SHERRY WEINTRAUB shared her angel story with me, I took a trip down to my family's condo in Florida. As a regular at the pool during my visits to Florida, many of the faces I see when I go to enjoy the un-New York-winter-like weather are familiar. During this particular trip, I had the pleasure of being introduced to a new face belonging to the inquisitive Rose Schena.

While jotting down my thoughts, Rose asked what I was working on. I explained my theory that all of our lives are like tapestries, emphasizing that what gives each of our individual tapestries their beauty are all the various threads, the influences of others, woven through them. And, I explained that I had been doing research into the influence of angels on each of our lives and how what I'd uncovered made me wonder about the sometimes hidden "true" identity of those around me.

Is that little girl with the Shirley Temple dimples and curly brown hair, the one whose smile lasted long after her mother pushed her stroller by my airport seat, more than another cute child? Is the woman at the tollbooth, the one who always gives me a hard time when my smallest bill is a twenty, a body of joy in disguise? Is that why I can't seem to resist the urge always to meet her gloom with a smile? Is the valet attendant, the one who said "nice book" and pointed to the angel book on my passenger seat as he handed me my keys, looking over more than just the care of my car?

And, I explained to Rose, the papers strewn out on my lawn chair were my jottings of memories I had of all the individuals who had given me the gift of their threads for my tapestry, individuals who I believed were each tools of angels, if not angels themselves.

Without judgment of my project, Rose offered the following prayer she often repeated during her childhood and so fondly regards even today:

> *"Angel dear, my guardian dear, to whom*
> *its love commits you near, ever this day be at my side*
> *to rule and guide, to rule and guard."*

Having never heard this prayer myself, but being extremely touched by Rose's interest and thoughtful words, I asked her if she would be gracious enough to write it down and leave it by my condo when she had a chance. I returned to New York soon after, and not having seen Rose again during my final days of vacation, and having become wrapped up in the hubbub surrounding all the other projects I was involved with at the time, I forgot about Rose's childhood recollection.

When I returned to Florida, however, Rose's thoughtfulness was manifested for me. While I had been away, she had slipped her prayer under my door. The amazing thing about this is that during my absence, my family's condo had work done on it. And despite the renovations and the cleaning team, Rose's prayer, written on what could easily have been mistaken as a scrap to be thrown away, survived.

This incident reaffirmed my belief that I was moving in the right direction with my study of angels. For some reason, once I started researching angels, they seemed to appear everywhere I turned. Within a few weeks of having received Rose's prayer, a colleague of mine, Henry Wurzer, volunteered the same prayer in the following rendition:

"Angel of God my Guardian dear, to whom His love commits me here, ever this day be at my side, to light and guard, to rule and guide."

I felt like a child learning a new rod after learning its meaning for the first time. I was amazed by all the places it seemed to appear. I had simply not been paying proper attention during the previous times I had heard about angels.

THE SOCIAL WORKER WITH HIDDEN WINGS

WHEN I WAS A CHILD there were a lot of words I had yet to learn. The most important three to my young ears came from the mouth of Mae Morse. She was tall and angular, with a rather hawkish, sculpted face topped with graying blonde hair. She was the social worker—the case professional assigned to my movement from my fourth foster home to my fifth. More importantly, she opened my life to possibility when, at the end of our first meeting, she leaned in close to me and said, "You are worthwhile."

My experience is that the child of the foster care system is often focused on survival and not development or sense of worth. Having grown up in five foster homes from the age of two, I began having a sense of myself as a person only when Mae Morse offered her insight to me at the age of eleven. When she said, "You are worthwhile," her words resonated within me like the pulse of my heartbeat. Perhaps that is why my earliest impression of our first meeting locks into the impression of a caring social worker doing more than duty required. By giving me a sense of self, she gave me a structure on which to build my life, my tapestry.

During that full year when she regularly came to check out my status, she reinforced the strength of my structure, my self-esteem, by continually saying those three kind words at the conclusion of each of our meetings. Mae Morse was infused with the spirit of an angel confirming not only mine, but every person's value in the sight of the Creator.

The influence of her message directly affected my capacity to develop a sense of self. Even today, I can hear her quietly whispering to my psyche, "*You are worthwhile.*"

> *"If we have listening ears, God speaks to us in our own language, whatever that language is."*
> —GANDHI

ANGELS HAVE, INDEED, brought messages to everyone open to them—from artists to businessmen. And, they've been called everything from good executive secretary to muse.

Former governor of Alaska, Walter Hickel, actually became famous during his last term as governor for attributing his inspiration for key decisions to his "little guy," his angel. It is not surprising then to find that the word angel is derived from the Greek word *angelos*, meaning messenger.

Beginning with Mae Morse, my life has been defined at every corner by the enlightening communication such messengers have delivered to me. I have often thought about why I have been so fortunate—why I was chosen to be on the receiving end of so many caring individuals. These messengers, my guardian angels, have been there to help me because I have been open to their presence, and not necessarily because I have been lucky and in the right place at the right time.

I've come to believe that, although Fate often seems to apportion seemingly uneven hands, we have all been dealt the gift of an individual who has the potential to turn our hand in life into a royal flush if we are open to him or her.

Although we cannot choose the threads of life given to us, we can select what we do with them. We can decide to discard the ugly immediately, or be open to more than a first impression, not playing into Fate's bluff.

SUMMER JOB

DURING THE SUMMER before my sophomore year of high school, in Watervliet, New York, the local newspaper carried an ad offering summer work at St. Agnes cemetery in the adjoining city, Menands, which also had the happy attribute of being situated on the bus line. As a young teenager, it was very exciting for me to contemplate my first full-time job, since my earlier stint was only as a part-time pinsetter at the Elk's Club bowling alley. As a member of a crew of six—one foreman and five green teenyboppers, my job was to help rake, mow, and tend to the cemetery grounds. The job is memorable not just for the joy of that first full-time paycheck, but also because the crew foreman, a leather-faced, regular year-round cemetery employee named Joel Salmon proved himself to be yet another thread in my tapestry.

Joel always chatted with the crew before we hopped on the flatbed trucks and moved out to the assigned sections. He would talk about the privilege we had to be the manicurists of grounds that were punctuated by so much grief, love and memory. Rather than having only a sense of a fairly low job in the hierarchy of the world of work, Joel would give a little homily about the idea that all work has a purpose, all work has dignity, and all work is worthwhile. By repeating that message every day of my teenage summer, he wove his powerful message into my tapestry of values. He helped me see the beauty in work that had originally been nothing more than a typical summer job.

> *"When a fellow begins to understand that he doesn't understand, he is beginning to understand."*
> —ANONYMOUS

ALTHOUGH RECENT STATISTICS report that 75 percent of Americans polled believe in angels, I did not initially ask everyone I know to share threads of their tapestries with me. Even though the number of "believers" is so high, I first only asked those I thought would be receptive to the idea. Because of this, I found myself in a situation in which a member of a group of colleagues I was meeting with asked how my study of angels was progressing. As the others we were with did not know about this pet project, I explained what I was doing. To my surprise, one of my colleagues, whom I have always had the deepest respect for as a no-nonsense executive, but who I never thought would be interested in sharing a story about an angelic influence, came forward in front of our entire group to share a piece of his tapestry with me. Although I was surprised, I was left with a feeling of contentment after hearing his story.

As was my experience with Joel Salmon, I realized again that things are not always as they seem to be. All my life I have known this, but repeatedly, I have found myself relearning this lesson. Sometimes some of the roughest threads, almost rope-like in texture, appear not to fit into our tapestry. Once added, they offer the expected endurance with the unexpected beauty of silk.

THE OFFICE MANAGER

JUST OUT OF HIGH SCHOOL, with no family, no money, no specific aspirations, my first full-time job was in the wholesale mattress department of Montgomery Ward as a "climber." That task involved climbing up the ladder bins, which held the mattresses segregated by alphabet and number. For example, C-7 would have a certain single bed piece, while the crosswalk ladder at the top would lead to a

B-7, which might be a queen size mattress. Simply scurrying about each shift up the ladder, over the crosswalk, and pushing mattress pieces called out by the floor foreman off the very high pile, to be caught in a soft trampoline, was not challenging, but was tiring as the day went by. It was around 4:00 p.m. on a Friday afternoon when hearing a C-7—rather than the desired B-7—my mattress got lift-off from me and, rather than landing on the trampoline, squashed the foreman straight on. His next two words were my first exposure to corporate consequence: GET OUT!

That night I went to a teenage dance and met a high school pal who asked what I was doing. "I was just fired from Montgomery Ward," I said, and then explained the story of C-7/B-7.

He told me he was the office boy in the circulation department at the Albany *Times Union* and was being promoted to clerk. He said if I came in Monday morning, he might be able to have me interviewed. However, he added, I looked very young and he thought it would be helpful if I wore a hat, a fedora. The next day I went to the Snappy Men's Shop on Central Avenue and bought my very first hat.

On Monday morning, I was inside the circulation department, application in hand, behind nine other guys who were also applying for the office boy job. There was no obvious urgency to that lowest job in the department. Thus, the office manager would only take applications in-between handling other chores. At least an hour and a half went by and there we stood, each individual interviewee slowly peeling off as he handed in his application. I was last in line.

When it came my turn, the office manager, Margaret Mahoney, a tiny woman about 4'10"—who at first glance closely resembled a pit bull—looked at me before taking my simple application and said, "I want to ask you a question." "Yes ma'am," I replied. After what seemed like another hour of staring at me she asked, "Why are you wearing that hat?" I explained that my friend suggested I looked too young and should wear a hat. "But," she admonished, "you have been INSIDE this department for over half an hour and are supposed to take your hat off when you are inside." I then whisked the hat off and told her I never had a hat before and did not know what to do. Her stern stare turned to a warm smile. To this day, I am convinced she gave me the job because I did not know enough to take my hat off.

More importantly, that diminutive lady had an angel spirit that gave her largeness of heart and soul, making her a vital thread of life in my personal tapestry.

She would tell us we were the ambassadors for the newspaper. "We," she would say, "are the first voices heard by a new subscriber or the last opportunities for an unhappy cancellation." Her mantra was that we should picture those customers as royalty—customer royalty was her everyday advocacy. She said, "If we picture those customers sitting on thrones with crowns on their heads, that mental picture will influence our tone of voice and leave an ambassador taste of goodwill for the paper."

I had not worked for that diminutive giant four months when she sat me down one Saturday morning during my shift and told me, "You are full of promise"—words I had never heard before. Her kind words provided the fuel to ignite an engine of higher purpose.

Indeed, as I went to college nights for six years, then off to Stanford University on a journalism fellowship, and then, nineteen years after walking in the door as the office boy, was named publisher of the Albany *Times Union*, I always heard the echo of Margaret Mahoney's encouraging words in my mind. In fact, when I first walked through the doors of the Hearst Corporate headquarters building to become the steward of all Hearst newspapers nationwide, I could hear Margaret saying, "You are full of promise."

The years have not dulled the early shining thread she brought to my tapestry. She was never the pit bull that my first impression saw her to be. In fact, my memory only sees the sweetness of her smile and the elfin smirk she exuded when a customer thanked her for the caring attention. Her smile, her smirk, her caring way were, I now realize, simply echoes of an angel whispering her excellence.

> *"Every blade of grass has an angel*
> *bending over it saying, 'Grow, Grow.'"*
> —THE TALMUD

AS I READ THROUGH all the angel threads that were sent to me, I continually found myself excited by the opening of each one, whether I was opening an email at my computer or trying to figure out the handwriting of a few friends and colleagues.

I could never quite stop being amazed by the individual capacity we each have to affect happiness in each other and the variety of ways we choose to do this. I was especially struck by the number of teachers who offered lessons past the usual reading and writing, instead emphasizing the life lessons their students needed to take their lives further.

THE GOLDEN VOICED GROCER

WHEN I WAS OFFICE BOY at the newspaper, I was also working part-time at a fruit and vegetable market owned by one Max Goldstein. Though Max had never finished grade school, he was an eloquent, compelling speaker, with an elegant dream in the way his voice could give wing to his future.

While I worked for him as a young teenager so open to the inspiration of others, I watched Max trudge through high school classes at night, then through college at night, and then to law school. He conquered the bar examination on the first try and then opened a store front law office, celebrating his diligence with a window-sized sign proclaiming, "Maxwell E. Goldstein, Attorney At Law."

Max, always tailored in his dusty brown hat, razor pant crease and selection of herringbone sports jackets, effervesced with style and vocal resonance. He was a constant advocate for growing into one's dreams—whatever those might be.

During his entire quest for higher education, Max continued to own and operate the fruit/vegetable store with the assistance of able managers. During that scholarly journey of his, he would always stop to volunteer a bit of philosophy to those of us who were what he called "graduate employees of the store," and who often came back to visit colleagues and even don an apron to help a customer or two.

Max had a shine to him. Whether seated nimbly on a wooden orange crate or in the handsome leather chair of his law office, where his store graduates would occasionally visit, he always took the time to encourage us. He would roll out that lovely resonant voice with each word like a sparkling gem, and always manage to pile those words so neatly that they seemed a verbal statue. For the long line of young, searching teenagers who were welcomed into Max's audience, his shine was the beacon drawing us to him again and again. He advocated stretch, reach, commitment and soaring aspirations, and would often conclude discussions with a reminder that it is a heaven-sent gift to be able to speak, to communicate our love for another, to encourage, to endorse, to guide, to celebrate success. "Never, ever," he would say, "waste the gift of speech on words that darken life or discourage people's potential."

Max Goldstein's golden words have never stopped ringing in my mind. I have long been convinced that Max had a true shine to him, a glow that seeped under that brown hat, through those pyramiding words, and into my personal tapestry. Max was a heaven-sent gift.

"The angelic realm supports our spiritual journey."

Spiritual Oasis

THE JOURNEY TO ARIEL
BY STEVAN J. THAYER

I have always, by nature, been inquisitive. As a youth, I would constantly take things apart and put then back together to gain a clear understanding of how they worked. As a young adult, I eagerly unleashed my inquisitiveness in the classroom, eventually earning a Master's degree in electrical engineering from Columbia University. When I began a 15-year career with Bell Telephone Laboratories in 1973, it was the realization of a dream. My days were soon filled with interesting projects that continually challenged me towards new discoveries. For years, I thrived on the tremendous intellectual stimulation I found at the Labs. I played the game well and was duly rewarded with patents, promotions and new projects to oversee. I even met my soulmate Carol at the Labs, and we entered into a wonderful marriage.

In time, the excitement of the dream began to wane, as a deep sense of dissatisfaction and emptiness rose from within.

I looked around and discovered that I had achieved my goal and had landed exactly where I had hoped to be. By the time I was in my mid-thirties, I had attained virtually everything I thought I had ever wanted, and yet my life seemed like it was becoming meaningless. My daily drive to work became a dreaded exercise. Instead of looking forward to each day, I had a deepening sense that I was about to waste yet another day of my life. I would catch myself feeling envious as I passed by the young men who were mowing lawns for a living. Free from any imposing structures, their lifestyle seemed strangely appealing.

To erase my discomfort, I immersed myself more fully in my work. I became extremely focused on my marriage and my hobbies of motorcycling and woodworking, so that no time was left to feel any pain. I decided to just hang on and endure my emptiness until I could retire.

THE WAKE-UP CALL

ONE DAY, a tragedy occurred. In an attempt to build team spirit, our laboratory had set up interdepartmental basketball games. During one game, my office mate was dribbling the ball down the court when he stumbled and fell. As he lay motionless on the floor, the players rushed to his side. At once, the gym became deafeningly silent.

My colleague had suffered a massive heat attack and died on the spot. He was three years away from retirement. I thought of the 17 years that stretched before me until my retirement date. In that moment, I knew that if I did not change my life's course, I would not make it to retirement.

Yet, the only future I could imagine was as an engineer at the Labs. I simply saw no other choices before me.

The environment at the Labs, however, became increasingly intense. The daily stress took its toll on me physically, and I developed serious illnesses that led to the need for repeated surgical interventions. I knew nothing at the time about the intimate interrelationship between the mind and body, and I was unaware that the level of stress I felt at work was in any way connected to my illnesses. Though it never occurred to me then, my illness was a powerful gift—a messenger for change.

THE COMMUNION

IN 1984, on the eve of my second surgery, I stood at the window of my hospital room and gazed at the fiery sun that was slowly sinking into the trees of Central Park. I became filled with fear as all the possible outcomes of my surgery played out in my mind. I reviewed the relative probabilities of each life-threatening scenario as described to me by the surgeon. I wondered if I would be around to see the next sunset.

As these terrifying thoughts raced through my head, I was suddenly overtaken by the most holy presence. The sensation was one of being outwardly paralyzed or frozen and inwardly pushed aside, as this powerful force entered my body. Through the top of my head, I felt something thick, like honey, pouring in and spreading slowly throughout my body. I could not stop it and did not want to stop it. For, as the presence slowly moved through me, I was lifted into the most indescribable state of ecstasy. I was filled with a pervasive sense of peace and all my fears dissolved. And I knew with absolute certainty that all would be well with the upcoming surgery. This understanding moved through me in an instant. I stood there, transfixed, when suddenly the knowledge "This is Jesus" flashed into my mind. I was filled to overflowing joy. I cannot explain how I knew, but I knew beyond all doubt that this indeed was Jesus.

I remained in this state of communion for some time. Then, as steadily and surely as Jesus had entered me, he left. Even after his presence was gone, I remained elevated in a state of pure spiritual ecstasy for the entire evening. The surgery did indeed go well. I healed quickly, returned to work at the Labs and spoke only to my wife about my communion experience.

AN EARTH ANGEL

ONE EVENING, at a dinner hosted by the Institute of Electrical and Electronic Engineers, I found myself seated next to Sandy, who was attending as the guest of another engineer. As we engaged in friendly conversation, I learned that she was a psychotherapist. I asked her about psychotherapy and confided in her about my feelings of emptiness at work. She gave me her business card and within a few days I had scheduled an appointment to come to her office.

When I arrived at Sandy's office, she led me to a seat in a comfortable room and asked me to tell her more about my feelings of emptiness. After about 15 minutes of listening to my story, she asked me if I knew that I was very sad. I had never thought of my life in those terms. I knew that I had been experiencing feelings of emptiness and even anger, but I could not identify with the notion of sadness. I began to wonder if I had wasted my time by coming to see Sandy, when she held her hand up in front of her and said simply, "Give me your sadness." This was just too much for my engineering mind to take. I decided to walk out of the session.

As my thoughts raced to determine whether or not I ought to pay Sandy for the wasted 15 minutes, I burst out in tears and cried from the depths of my being. I could not stop, but I had no idea what I was crying about. After several minutes, Sandy lowered her hand and said, "That's enough for now." As she did that, I stopped crying. I felt as though a heavy burden had been lifted off of me, and I felt wonderful.

From my newfound state of expanded well-being, I asked Sandy to tell me what had just taken place. She explained that she had used an energy therapy technique to release my sadness.

While I had never heard of energy therapy, I knew that this had been a life-altering experience and I wanted to know more. It is clear to me that Sandy had entered my experience as an *Earth Angel*. Our meeting was not a random event thrown together by a random Universe; Sandy had come to convey a life-changing message that was essential to my soul's growth.

Because I was astounded by the healing power energy therapy held for me, I was driven to master the energy therapy skills that would allow me to help others in the same powerful way that Sandy had helped me. As I studied, I learned that the human body has an electromagnetic field that stores suppressed feelings. I discovered that I could now use my engineering skills, focused through energy therapy, to act as a catalyst for healing in the lives of others. I took many classes and read countless books on energy therapy, and eventually I became a certified energy therapy teacher.

In the fall of 1988, with tremendous love, support and even insistence from my wife, Carol, I resigned from my position with the Labs, and saw a new dream begin to unfold when I founded "The Center Of Being," a holistic health center. I began a full-time energy therapy and teaching practice. Within the first year of opening my center, my calendar was full. I was not only living in a creative state of joy, but I now sensed that I was deeply attuned to my life's true purpose.

I began seeing the manifestation of my life's fullest potential. Over several years, I made exciting new discoveries in the field of energy therapy, which evolved into a new healing system I call Integrated Energy Therapy®. Every day, I was given the opportunity to assist extraordinary people as they healed physical and emotional challenges. Through the remarkable power of IET, I saw problems resolving and illnesses dissipating. I soon began to teach IET to others who thirsted for this information and experienced the pure joy of watching its power work through their hands as well. This was a far cry from the emptiness I felt at the Labs. It seemed that life couldn't get better than this.

Meeting An Angel

IT WAS THE SUMMER of 1993, and my energy therapy practice was growing steadily. One afternoon, as a client relaxed on the energy table, I began channeling energy into the area of her throat. Suddenly, I sensed the presence of someone standing behind me. I turned and saw no one, yet an unmistakable feeling of heat and pressure began to flow through me. The feeling instantly triggered a powerful memory of my mystical experience in the hospital. We both felt a powerful energetic shift occurring.

"What's happening?" my client asked. I paused for a moment as I searched for words to adequately explain what I was feeling. At once, a wave of love washed over me and intensified as distinct words formed in my mind. "We have come to help you." I spoke these words aloud to my client, who then asked, "What is your name?" "We don't have names," was the clear response that I heard and repeated. My client continued, "Then, what name can I use to call upon you in the future?" The answer came quickly, "Names will not be necessary. We will hear you and be with you." But my client persisted, "I need to have a name to be able to know it is you." There was silence, and then I clearly "heard" the name *Ariel*.

Ariel then spoke through me, to my client, about the traumas in my client's past. The immeasurable poignancy of these heartfelt messages combined with the incredible healing energy flowing through me, and elevated both my client and myself to a state of tearful exuberance.

There's An Angel
In Your Waiting Room

SEVERAL DAYS LATER, another client, who knew nothing about my experience with *Ariel*, appeared flushed with excitement as she entered my office. "You aren't going to believe this," she exclaimed, "but you have an angel in your waiting room!" Although I had seen great shifts and changes in my beliefs since my days as an engineer, the notion of "winged beings of light" was just too much. I did not believe in angels, let alone consider that one actually could be seen in my waiting room. I seriously wondered if my client was having a hallucinatory experience.

Undaunted by my less than enthusiastic response, my effusive client went on to tell me that the angel in my waiting room was particularly large, at least 8-feet tall and, in fact, donned wonderful, glowing wings. She then told me that the angel had also spoken to her. "The angel wants you to know that she is your angel and has come to work with you."

Now my tolerance was being pushed to its absolute limit. What next? I thought to myself, trying not to appear agitated. Now, angels are conversing with my clients in my waiting room!

She continued the angel's message, "The angel wants you to know that her name is *Ariel*." In that moment, reality as I knew it completely shattered. It was as though a cosmic trap door had opened below me and I had fallen through. A chill ran up my spine, as I suddenly understood that *Ariel* was actually an angel.

Since that day, *Ariel* has worked through me to teach and heal countless individuals. She continues to bring the energy of the angelic realm to support my personal spiritual journey as well. I have come to understand that *Ariel* serves God though assisting people to see beyond their perceived limitations. The purity of her love and wisdom helps individuals to deepen their personal relationship with the Divine and strengthens their understanding of their soul's purpose. While *Ariel* unceasingly supports the lives of individuals, she also holds a broader intention to touch all the people of the Earth with the truth that we live in a loving and abundant Universe.

Little Angel

There's a little angel
Out there, somewhere
Looking down on me
And giving me love and care

This little angel
Will help me get by
All of my troubles
And help me soar and fly

This little angel
Will come and go
Tell me little things
That I'd never know

This little angel
Will keep me alive
This little angel
Gives me special vibes

This little angel
Will always be here for me
This little angel
Is one thing, I can only see

This little angel
Shines on me with its light
Giving me a message
To not do wrong, but right

This little angel
Brings the life out of me
Protects me
Which lets me be free

—Shantel Johnson

Inspiration

Writer's block. I don't know of one person who has not been hit by this problem, be it for a simple congratulatory greeting on a birthday card; a term paper, a resume cover letter; or even something as large as a full-fledged novel. For whatever reason, even if we have an idea of what we want to say, we occasionally have a difficult time saying it. Sometimes the first sentence is all that is really needed to get started. Other times, though, when we are not even sure of where we want to go, more is needed. This is where inspiration comes in.

Whether we have an idea of where we are headed or not, inspiration is what gives us a jumpstart. Just as we feel as though our stalled situation is going to turn into a complete breakdown, inspiration comes along to offer a helping hand. In all areas of life, not just writer's block, inspiration sparks our get-go. It offers us a first sense to roll with another thread for our tapestry.

Unfortunately, inspiration doesn't have a day-planner; you can't just schedule a servicing whenever you are in need of it. Because of this, you might find yourself waiting for that burst of adrenaline that gets your motor running. Luckily, although it doesn't have a set schedule, it is present all the time. The trick is to figure out what you have to do to access it. For some artists, the key to their inspiration strongbox lies in the accomplishments of others. Sometimes reading about or seeing what others have done reminds them how to unlock their inspiration. In many instances, others provide the access key nudging an inexplicable ignition of our inspiration. A whisper touches our inspiration start button.

A Literate Shipmate

Having been called to serve in the U.S. Navy during the Korean conflict, I left the Albany *Times Union* to go to radio training school. Upon graduation, I was assigned to a rescue and salvage vessel, the USS Recovery, which had the happy position of being anchored at the Brooklyn Navy yard, just 150 miles from my Albany, New York, hometown. As the ship had not moved in seven years, I was told I could expect a land-based tenure for my remaining naval service.

That promise was short lived though. Less than an hour after I stepped aboard, the ship gave out the three-toot signal indicating it was leaving the dock for sea. My shipmates were cheered by the idea of actual sea duty, but I was grim about the notion of bouncing around a vast ocean for the next few years, having little to entertain myself with. I was in limbo and hadn't figured out how to get out of it yet.

Assigned to my duty station on the bridge of the ship, where the radio shack was located, I approached my sea bound assignment with distress and confusion. Also assigned by random drawing to my bunk, a slim strip of canvas just wide enough for an average body size, I found myself in the middle between an upper and lower. The shipmate assigned the bunk above me was also, I noticed, one of the sailors working on the bridge of the ship. His name was Bob Myers. As we began to get to know each other, he told me had joined the Navy after graduating from New York University with an honor degree in English Literature. Bob told me he chose to be an enlisted man rather than the officer his college background entitled him to, because he wanted to taste the life of a team member rather than a team official.

Bob had negotiated for two lockers near our bunks and the second, I came to see, was filled with all the classics—Blake, Milton, Homer, Shakespeare, and just about every other author in the Modern Library series.

With my learning deprived foster home background and truly minimal devotion to school or intellect, it seemed very natural and honest to tell Bob—as he opened that personal library he had jammed in his tiny locker—that I had never read a complete book. Instead of looking down his nose from his top bunk at me, Bob took it upon himself to educate me. For reasons unknown to me, Bob told me that he would adopt me as a reader/student if I would be genuinely open to learning. Thus began my education "abroad."

Bob would have me read one of the great novels, and then follow-up with hours of fascinating time talking with me about character development, plot nuance, and the writing style of each great work's author. I had no idea where I was going with the information Bob gave me. I just knew that I enjoyed his teaching.

He introduced me to worlds and people far removed from my previous experiences. He taught me how to let the author guide my imagination. He gave me a place to start and inspired me to do something with the structure my social worker, Mae Morse, had years earlier set for me. He illuminated my perspective through countless classic books and taught me to revere the unique gift an author can provide a reader.

By the time I left the USS Recovery, I had the privilege of a passionate guided tour through a vast collection of many of the world's great books. When I then entered Siena College and chose to be an English major, I was a star student. My grades were, I knew then and I know now, simply a reflection of the unique inspirational threads that were woven into my spirit by Bob Myers being in the bunk above me; having the great novels in his second locker; and choosing to become an instrument of instruction for me.

When I was making those good grades, although it was I who wanted to make the grades, it was the passion Bob ignited in my soul for literature that made it possible. Interestingly, as I pen these thoughts recalling Bob, I also recall how gentle was his voice, his manner, his character—and how absolute he was as a clear leader on the bridge of that ship.

Although I did not choose my bunkmate, his literary insight and devotion, his taking on a student, or his memorable character, someone else did. I am persuaded that my bunkmate, Bob Myers, was a willing vessel for a guiding spirit to inspire my mind's eye to see the beauty and possibility of each person's more noble prospects. Somehow, I am most comforted by the idea that the guiding spirit infused through Bob was a smiling angel.

AS WAS MY EXPERIENCE with Bob Myers, it sometimes takes someone else's acknowledging your potential for you to see the same in yourself.

Do you remember the children's story of the ugliest duckling? As the story is told, a baby swan finds himself being raised as a duckling, with no other swans in sight. As he grows up, he is made fun of and laughed at for being different from all the other ducklings. The short ending to this endearing tale is that this ugly duckling one day finds out that he is a beautiful swan—one of the most beautiful and graceful creatures in the entire world. Because he had been continually told he was ugly, he was unable to see his own beauty. It was not until this quality was pointed out to him that he realized it.

Like Bob Myers helping me to establish a course for my life by bringing my potential to my attention, many of the angel threads sent to me have described similar individuals. One such story came from John Telfer, editor of the *Midland* (Michigan) *Daily News*.

One Person's Words Make a Difference
by John Telfer

A SHORT PROGRAM ON an arena radio station brought back memories about the dangers of placing labels on people. The program was talking about how some people had been approached by an old man selling produce. The man had glazed-over eyes and white stubble on his face. The people bought something from him as quickly as they could so he would leave. They had labeled him a dirty wino because of his appearance and the look in his eyes.

He kept coming around and in time they learned he was not a drunk after all; his eyes were glazed over by cataracts. People had judged this man without knowledge, or very little knowledge, of who he was. If we are honest, we all have done the same thing. And some of us have been victims of such judgment.

A few years ago, I had an opportunity to speak to the students of Central Middle School. I gave them a small glimpse of the path I took to becoming editor of the *Daily News*. I am not sure how teachers and administrators reacted to the message, because success stories don't always come about in ways people expect.

For example, when I was the age of those Central Middle School students, my favorite class was gym. I had a teacher who could not control his class, suffered a nervous breakdown and left the profession. In this environment, it was hard to enjoy school and I didn't.

High school was even more of a letdown. At one point, a counselor told my mother I would never amount to anything. With that label being reinforced daily, they were right. While at high school, I did only what was necessary to pass classes. No homework. No cramming for exams. I lived up to the expectations of that high school counselor and my teachers.

Graduation day provided a new opportunity, a clean slate. But I had to go to a junior college because my high school grades were so poor, and I had no idea what I wanted to do anyway. One of the classes I took my first year was a writing class. I had always enjoyed writing, but never pursued it. The instructor, a reporter at the local newspaper, told me I had talent and should see if I could do some reporting work at the college newspaper.

Those were the first positive and supportive words spoken to me by an instructor since fifth grade. The last year school was fun; the label had changed. The next thing you know, I was working at the college newspaper. I was getting straight A's in my classes. Teachers began communicating with me in a manner that showed respect.

I transferred to Central Michigan University, and the success continued. I graduated with honors, having worked as a reporter and an editor at the university newspaper. Two professional papers, three jobs and 13 years later, I arrived at the *Daily News*.

Along the way, I never stopped learning, and my love for writing, for knowledge and for people never dimmed. Was it because of those positive words from that instructor 20-plus years ago? At the time, I would not have believed it; but looking back now, I can clearly see that class and that instructor were turning points in my life and my career.

I shudder to think what might have occurred had someone not finally decided to judge me for the person they thought I could be. That's what labels do. They block your ability to see anything but preconceived notions, much like the people who thought the old man was a wino. The biggest problem with labels is they can stick for a lifetime. Not everybody gets a second chance. And that's a shame.

Think about it the next time you are tempted to place a label on some child or an adult you know. Instead of calling them a troublemaker or a disruptive influence, try some encouraging words. You might change a life.

"Passion is the drunkenness of the mind."
–ROBERT SOUTH

NORMAN VINCENT PEALE once said, "Your enthusiasm will be infectious, stimulating and attractive to others. They will love you for it. They will go for you and with you." He was right.

Have you ever been so enthusiastic, so passionate about something that the words "stop and go" cease to exist? You feel like a volcano about to explode, so you continue until you burst forth with excitement. Have you noticed that when you are turning out this energy, you inspire yourself to do more and go in new directions? Instead of coming to an end after each accomplishment, you find yourself arriving at a new beginning, inspiring others to go with you.

I've tried to give excellence to everything I do, but of all the things I have been inspired to do, I have found that passion is the overriding factor dictating how far I go. I surpass excellence and even perfection when passion is at the helm.

PARADISE LOST AND FOUND

IT WAS JUST ONE more course offered in the catalog for English majors at Siena College, where I was spending evenings in pursuit of an undergraduate degree. Milton's *Paradise Lost* was the course name and Father Amadeus, the professor's. The course was amenable to my schedule and thus was inviting.

On the first night of instruction, the medium height, wavy haired Franciscan swept into the classroom in full-length brown robes flowing just to the tops of his open-toed sandals. His ruddy complexion beamed as he told us he was there to cause us to love the majesty of Milton and his greatest work. Wasting no time on the administrative niceties of student names, etc., Father told us he simply trusted that we would be in attendance, show up for tests, and do the reading and homework. His mission, he said, was to pack every moment of every class with his enthusiasm for the major talent of Milton.

Indeed, robe flowing reluctantly behind him, trying to keep up, he circled the classroom, darting from side to side like a hummingbird, pausing long enough to permit a quick glance before his passion-fueled energy bounded off on another explanation of the genius of Milton. Within very few classes, I found myself as anxious to attend his class as a newborn for the evening feeding; I could barely wait for my ears to be filled with the Milton advocacy he wove so brilliantly. In fact, many of my classmates and I joked about the fact that, were it permitted, we would simply major in Milton and forego all other required courses.

Often my schedule permitted me to arrive at Siena College an hour or so prior to my first class. On occasion, I would stop at the chapel for a period of meditation. Sometimes, I would be in that chapel when Franciscan priests would gather in community behind a decorative screen at the rear of the altar and sing Franciscan chants. Although there were dozens of them in those occasional hidden choirs, I always believed I could detect the song of Father Amadeus (later known as Father Peter Fiore after the vernacular name changes advocated in his order) punctuating the many voices—just as he punctuated the classroom with his brilliant lessons, insights, purpose and circumstance of Milton's *Paradise Lost.*

What Father Amadeus gave every student was an affirmation that if one brings passion to what he or she does, that passion can permeate the air, punctuating the power of the moment with an unforgettable exclamation mark. I still wonder what or who it was that made Father Amadeus's Milton message resonate beyond the literary achievement and make the lesson of passionate love for his vocation be the lasting thread. Perhaps, just perhaps, it was an angel Milton fan who decided that this passionate Franciscan was a ready vehicle to bring the larger message of learning shared passionately.

MARIAN TANNER, THE MODEL for the life-loving effervescent character, Auntie Mame, was once described as having "lived in capital letters." What a wonderful description!

There can be no mistaking the energy such a person must have! Father Peter Fiore had such energy. He also lived life in "capital letters." The passion he first introduced to me has remained with me through the years because of this—and because I have found his same enthusiasm for the good things in life alive in my mother-in-law, Lilly Brady.

When I finally sat down to put together *Angel Threads,* Lilly was one of the first persons I thought of to talk to. Lilly has been a potent thread in the lives of so many she has touched in her nine decades. She is always positive, always seeking the next adventure, always growing by taking classes. In fact, when I first sat down to discuss *Angel Threads* with her, she was attending St. Rose College at the young age of 92, but according to her, "only auditing the classes for fun."

Her remarkable spirit has made her a caring mother, grandmother, great-grandmother, and, for me, an inspiring mother-in-law. Lilly's ability to seek out the enjoyment and let the rest go by has always reminded me of the following line in Milton's *Paradise Lost*: "The mind is its own place, and in itself can make a heaven of hell and a hell of heaven."

The Ladder to Steerage
by Lilly Brady

As a young teenager, I was sent a ticket by my Aunt Jane to travel from my native Ireland to America, where I could establish myself as a new citizen. The trip would take almost three weeks aboard a massive ship packed with Irish folk chasing their dreams to a new land. Once aboard ship, and waving farewell to my family on the Dublin docks, I was told my ticket was for steerage level, but as all the space was taken, I would be placed on the more spacious second-class level. The second-class passengers were an older, more serious lot, which made the densely packed steerage, whose passengers' jovial songs drifted to the decks above, more tempting to me and the roommate I had been assigned, Anna.

By the third day, Anna discovered a steep ladder down to steerage. Only teenagers, we winked at the sailor guarding the ladder, deflecting his attention, and climbed down to rousing song welcoming us from the upper deck. We jigged all the day long. When we later returned to the second-class area for dinner, we found ourselves being criticized for mingling with the "low-life" folk in steerage. Those who complained were all characterized by a common plague of boredom. They stood in true contrast to the boisterous singing, dancing celebrators of life on the lowest deck.

Anna was my everyday soulmate on the ship. Without her invitation, I most likely would not have had the courage to climb that steep ladder to steerage. Anna taught me to savor the enjoyment and look past the sweaty, grimy, cramped quarters. I began then and there to notice that I had a great capacity for enjoyment, and I decided never to let the small irritations detract from my enjoyment.

When the ship landed at the docks of New York, Anna and I embraced and went our separate ways. Although I never was to see Anna again, I never forgot how she opened my mind and soul to a life of enjoyment.

"The secret of success is constancy of purpose."
–Benjamin Disraeli

"WHEN ARE WE GOING TO GET THERE?" Anyone who has spent time with children knows this infamous question to be a staple of family vacations: It usually starts about fifteen minutes into a ten hour drive and follows every five minutes thereafter. And what keeps us from turning around and heading for home when our beloved children in the back seats of our overly packed cars add a whine, and for those of us lucky to have more than one child, a round of "When are we going to get there's?"–each starting where the other left off? Purpose.

Purpose defines our final destination; it offers an outline for our goals—something we cannot always see from a distance. Thus, it keeps us going. And the reason it keeps us going is that, along with passion, purpose is a catalyst for inspiration. It inspires us to come up with clever ideas and games to keep our families happy and our patience balanced while we drive forward.

In every aspect of life, it is important to have a series of destinations to arrive at. It is not necessary to have one final goal, as this may change along the way, but it is important to have small rest points on our path to arrive at by the end of the day. Having purpose—something to look forward to—and passion—a love for what you are doing—will inspire you to get there, wherever there may be.

A Partner/Boss

Angelo monaco, Angie to everyone, had purpose. He was the retail-advertising manager of the Albany *Times Union* when I first joined the ad sales staff. Angie had a face that looked as if it would be a candidate to be chiseled into a mountainside—deep lines, a permanent frown, and a long oval face, topping a neck which looked to be very reluctantly framed in a shirt and necktie. My most vivid memory of his dress was a blue/white seersucker suit struggling to stay on his wrestler body. Angie looked and acted like a man's man. Although I never saw him smoke a cigarette, neither did I see him without a long, black, ivory-tipped cigarette holder in his lips. It seemed more prop than habit and had the desired effect of causing one to look at his lips carefully when his low-pitched voice was whispering some instruction through and around that cigarette holder. Intimidation seemed his ally for any who had a direct reporting relationship to him.

Extremely focused on the design he had planned for our advertising department, he had no patience for foolish mistakes or sluggish performances. I can vividly recall his daily ritual of going though the competing afternoon newspaper at the end of every day and seeking an extemporaneous explanation for the ad rep assigned to an account not advertising in our *Times Union*. No ad rep wanted to come to a second day of such revelation without having made the effort to make the sale. Tough, Humphrey Bogart-like Angie would dangle that cigarette holder and stare down any lapsed salesperson with lips poised somewhere between a smile implying "try me on for size" and a look of utter dismay. Everyone wanted to perform for this gruff, rumpled, no-nonsense, fierce competitor. It was the "fierce competitor" in us that he encouraged above all else if the world of commerce and business was to remain our arena.

My sales territory was the grocery stores. A major account was the A&P chain, which favored our *Times Union* only slightly as we had a Sunday newspaper and our competitor did not. The Albany area had been chosen to be the opening place for the first A&P Superstore. All the national executives were to be in Albany for the Monday morning opening. Kick-off for the event was to be a two-page ad in our Sunday *Times Union*. I handled the account, processed the ad and was frankly pumped up with pride at our coup of having the launch exclusively in our newspaper—an emotional high.

On Sunday morning I raced to get the paper and flipped pages looking for the colorful opening ads for the new Superstore. No ad. Sinking feeling. Disaster looming in my imagination, I drove to the newspaper plant and talked to the composing room foreman, who then chased down the original copy. The insertion date for the ad to run—in my clear handwriting—was for the following Sunday. I had scheduled the ad for the biggest event in A&P history for the wrong Sunday. I wandered out of the plant devastated, confused and certain my career was over. Almost without thinking, I drove to the home of Angie Monaco, who was just returning from church with his family, and who had not yet been through the Sunday paper. I burst out in a shriek that I had mis-scheduled the major opening.

Angie leaned against the car, slowly took out his cigarette holder, managed that slim lipped grin/smirk and said, "You cannot be telling me you left the ad out of the paper, can you?" "Yes," I answered. With that, he waved his arm, beckoning me to follow him into the house. Once inside, he picked up the telephone and asked for the home number and address of Jack Casey, the A&P regional manager. With address in hand, he stormed out of the house, barely giving me enough time to follow, and we drove to Jack Casey's home. Angie rang the bell, and when Jack answered, he told him what I had done. They both stared at me and then Angie said, "We are here to start over and get our four pages of opening announcements in the Monday morning paper—in the first section, two pages in the second section, all without charge to A & P." Jack agreed with the remedy and the three of us set off to the newspaper to make the arrangements.

On the drive down, Angie said to Jack Casey that we must keep in mind that the only reason A&P's opening day could be saved by running the double impact ads on Monday was because I had owned up, sought him out, and acted like a partner more than an employee. Jack agreed. Later that day a fruit basket arrived at my home with a message from Jack: "You Saved The Day Partner. Thank You!"

On Monday I told Angie of the basket. He smiled full face for the first time I could ever recall and said that the life lesson for me was always to step up to the plate when a mistake happened and when the opportunity came my way, to always treat an honest employee/colleague as a partner. When one's purpose is clear, the largest mistakes can often be cleared up with what feels like a little effort. What feels like a mistake is really a new lesson. Angie gave me an insight that has remained with me throughout my career. He was an angel that day—a thread in my tapestry, a partner in life.

HAVE YOU EVER NOTICED that sometimes when you think you are on the right track with your tapestry, the thread you are pulling through knots up on the backside and no matter how hard you try, it seems to become more and more tangled, until you begin to feel as though you made a mistake? And then, out of nowhere, have you also noticed that after trying just about everything, when you are on the verge of giving up, the knot suddenly loosens and the thread slides through? Not giving up is what allowed this to happen.

When Angie Monaco introduced me to the importance of purpose—of having a reason for doing the things I did, he introduced me to the concept of never giving up. Likewise, a friend and colleague of mine, *Parade* magazine editor, Walter Anderson, had a similar experience growing up.

"YOU CAN DO THIS"
FOUR WORDS AND ONE UNFORGETTABLE WOMAN
—THEY CHANGED MY LIFE
BY WALTER ANDERSON

BARRY WILLIAMS WAS MY best friend when I was growing up in White Plains. In many ways, our lives were completely

e lived in a two-story clapboard with a back-
ily occupied a railroad flat in a tenement build-
he life was troubled; his seemed serene. He was
black; I m white. I dropped out of high school; he went
on to Harvard. But what we had in common, what made
all the difference in the world to me, was Barry's mother,
Mrs. Williams.

I didn't even know her first name. She was always Mrs.
Williams, the tall, dignified schoolteacher across the street,
who was rearing three sons on her own.

Sometimes Mrs. Williams told us stories. "A long time
ago, in the marsh country of England, there lived an or-
phan boy named Pip," she might say. "One bleak evening,
he was visiting the graves of his parents. The sky darkened,
and the wind blew, and the boy, afraid, started crying. Suddenly a deep voice roared, 'Keep still or I'll cut your throat!'
and a terrible figure rose from among the tombstones."

"Then what happened?" I asked enthralled.

"If you'd like to know," she answered, smiling, "read
the book *Great Expectations* by Charles Dickens." She made
me want to go to the library.

Other times Barry and I would be out in the driveway
on a Saturday shooting hoops, and his mother would say,
"Boys, could you come and give me a hand?" The next thing
we knew, we would be helping her with a student she was
tutoring. I felt proud that Mrs. Williams valued my help. I
didn't realize until much later that by teaching someone
else, Barry and I were learning too.

Mrs. Williams made sure that Barry and his brothers
did their homework, and if I happened to be visiting, she

watched while I did mine. Usually Barry and I studied at the kitchen table. Mrs. Williams stayed nearby, in case we had a question. At home I lived in fear of my father's alcoholic rages, and I wasn't used to that kind of discipline or attention.

Her favorite words of encouragement were: "You can do this." I heard them often because I was impatient and easily frustrated. When a math problem refused to yield its secret or an essay had me confounded, I gave up and slammed my pencil on the table. Calmly, Mrs. Williams took a seat beside me and talked me through the assignment step-by-step. Something about her quiet reassurance, "You can do this, Walter," settled me down, and I managed to finish my work.

Barry and his brothers went to private schools, an expense that must have strained Mrs. William's budget, and she worried about the quality of my education. One day she took me to a local parochial school, had me tested, then persuaded my parents to let me change schools.

I attended for a while, but after an angry exchange with a teacher I was told not to return. Unperturbed, Mrs. Williams took me to another school, had me tested again, made sure I would receive the necessary financial assistance, then convinced my parents that it was important for my future. I made it through two grades in one year.

When we were ready for high school, Barry applied to boarding schools. Mrs. Williams believed that would be the best thing for me as well. Anything to get me away from the streets, where she saw too many kids getting into trouble. I was accepted into a prep school and again awarded a scholarship. But when I saw the other students—kids in pressed shirts and blazers—all my old insecurities came rushing back. I couldn't do it. I entered the high school in town. A year and a half later, failing nearly every subject, I dropped out.

One of the hardest things I've ever had to do was tell Mrs. Williams. She gazed at me with her cool brown eyes and said nothing. "I'm going into the Marines," I said shrugging, "I won't need high school."

"Okay, Walter." Her voice was quiet, resigned. "I don't agree with you, but you're old enough to make your own decisions."

Six months later, in the Marines, I realized how right she was. In three and a half years I would be out of the service, a 21-year-old with no diploma. What sort of future would I have? *Dear Lord,* I prayed, *please give me another chance.*

The next morning, I went to the First Sergeant and said, "I want to go to school." The first step was to take an exam for a high school equivalency diploma. I must have done well because after seeing my scores the Marines enrolled me in a special electronics program.

Again, I felt out of my league. *Dear God,* I prayed, let *me pass just one course.* The instructor began his lecture. I started taking notes, but there was so much I didn't know; so much I was afraid I would never know. There's no way I'll get through this class I thought, putting my pen down. I should just walk out the door right now.

All at once, I heard a familiar voice inside my head, warm and reassuring: "Don't give up Walter. You can do this." I wasn't so sure, but I owed it to Mrs. Williams and to myself to try. Taking a deep breath, I picked up my pen and concentrated on my instructor's lecture.

I graduated seventh in a class of 24. It was the biggest thrill of my life. I can't wait to tell Mrs. Williams, I thought. But by the time I made it back home the Williamses were not living across the street anymore. They had moved and no one knew their new address.

After the Marines, I went on to receive my bachelor's degree. By the age of 26, I was well into a career in journalism. I became a newspaper editor and eventually editor-in-chief of *Parade* magazine.

Several years ago when I spoke at a dinner, I told the audience, "All the successful people I've ever known have one thing in common. In their childhood, there was someone who said, "I believe in you." For me, that was my best friend's mother, Mrs. Williams."

It was gratifying to give her credit. Still, I longed to tell her how she had changed my life and thank her for all she had done for me.

Some time later, I spoke to Parade's senior investigative reporter about Mrs. Williams. "I wish I could get in touch with her," I said.

"I can find her," he declared.

A few days later he called. "Walter, Mrs. Williams lives a few miles away from you," he said. " She's retired from teaching and her son Barry is a successful attorney."

Mrs. Williams and I had a reunion at my house. All I could do at first was thank her over and over again. Then the words spilled out in a rush, as I told her about everything I had accomplished, eager to make her proud.

"I graduated college as valedictorian. Then I got into journalism, and today I am the editor-in-chief of a magazine."

She game me a smile. "Of course, you are, Walter," She said, her voice as full of assurance as it had been so many years ago. Ilza Louise Berry Williams never doubted for a moment I could accomplish anything I set my mind to. It just took me awhile to believe it for myself.

Spiritual Oasis

Journey to Divine Guidance
by Doreen Virtue, Ph.D.

M y mother, a Christian spiritual healer, introduced me to Divine Guidance when I was very small. She taught me to turn to God to resolve all sorts of situations. I learned that God spoke to me throughout the day, and all I needed to do was listen. Sometimes, God's voice would be audible. For instance, when I was eight-years-old and leaving Sunday school, I heard a male voice outside my right ear. This voice told me with loving firmness that my life mission involved teaching others about the connection between the mind and body.

Sometimes we are afraid because what God guides us to do seems intimidating. This was especially true when I was in my early twenties. I had married right out of high school and had two sons. While I was very happy to have children, I still felt that something important was missing in my life. I wanted to contribute to the world and have a meaningful career. Yet I could not imagine what I could offer to others that would make a difference. After all, I had no unique ideas, formal education, or special training.

At some level, I was praying to God for guidance. Although these were not conscious prayers, I remember thinking, "*God please help me!*" and singing hymns such as, "Shepherd, Show Me How to Go."

In my own way, I asked for Divine guidance. After all, Divine guidance is an answer to our prayers, or the prayers others have said on our behalf. Whenever we ask heaven to help, we receive assistance. Sometimes the help is direct, as when an angel intervenes in a lifesaving incident. More often, though, God answers our prayers by giving practical advice.

I received His guidance one day while tending the small garden next to our condominium. I had always noticed that gardening put me into a meditative mindset that allowed me to transcend negative thinking. As I pulled weeds that day, I had a mental vision that reminded me of watching a black-and-white movie in a penny arcade. In this vision, I saw myself enjoying a very different life. I was a published author, helping and healing others and enjoying life. I knew that my vision was not a simple daydream, because it made me so uncomfortable. After all, I didn't think I had what it took to write books and help others.

I tried to ignore the visions, but they continued to arrive daily. Soon, they were full-color movies, complete with details about my life. One would think these images would be a pleasant escape from an uncomfortable life, yet they actually made me feel worse about myself. I began to feel haunted and chased by the visions.

Accidentally, I discovered that if I ate a large meal, I could stop the movie. Therefore, I began eating a lot of food. After a few months, I'd gained many extra pounds and was no happier with my life or myself. Every time my food would digest, I would receive the visions and accompanying feelings that urged me to write books and become a healer. I finally tired of using food to obstruct my mental movies. At that point, I surrendered and asked God to help me.

"*I am very frightened,*" I admitted to God and myself. "*I would love to have the life that You keep showing me, but I have no idea how I could do any of those things. I mean, I don't have much time or money. I am not sure I am smart enough to write books, and I do not know much about the publishing industry. But if this is what You want me to do, I will follow Your lead.*"

After committing to God and asking for guidance, I received a strong impression that came as a gut feeling and intellectual knowingness. I knew and felt that I was supposed to call my local college's admissions counselor. *I do not know how I will have the time, money, or intelligence to get through school,* I mentally told God. *However, I did promise that I would trust and follow your lead.*

When I completed the first step and called the admissions counselor, I received another impression that said, *Make an appointment to see the counselor in person.* Again, I initially resisted, but remembered my promise to God. Despite my reservations, I found myself enrolling in college exactly as God had led me to do. Since my husband worked a late-shift, he agreed to watch our young children while I attended school. Then I'd come home before he went to work.

The Divine guidance led me along one step at a time until, very quickly, all of the visions in my mental movie had come true. God provided all the money, ideas, and information I needed. I earned two degrees from one of the country's most expensive private universities.

If I had waited for God to "show me the money" first, I would still be waiting! Yet, by walking in faith that God would provide, I received all of my material support. By the time I was 30, I was a psychotherapist and bestselling author traveling the lecture and talk show circuit.

In retrospect, I now understand that God guides us in successive baby steps. We must be aware of the tiny bits of guidance, and then complete them, before we receive the next step in our guidance. I had felt stuck and frightened because I could not map out how I could accomplish the things I saw in my visions.

Essentially, I had wanted God to hand me a full blueprint for how He intended me to succeed, with full assurance that I would agree to move forward. Still, I am glad God did not show me the entire plan ahead of time. If He had shown me, for instance, that I would be traveling to New York City all by myself late at night during my travels, I probably would have said, "No way!" I also found that the HOW of my life plan was up to God. In ways I could never have planned or controlled, I received enough time, money, and intelligence to accomplish my Divine mission.

Direction

"If we knew we were on the right road, having to leave it would mean endless despair. But we are on a road that only leads to a second one and then to a third one and so forth. And the real highway will not be sighted for a long, long time, perhaps never. So we drift in doubt. But also in an unbelievable diversity. Thus the accomplishment of hopes remains an always unexpected miracle. But in compensation, the miracle remains forever possible."
—FRANK KAFKA

Imagine you have a 10,000-piece jigsaw puzzle to put together, but no box top indicating what the finished puzzle looks like. What do you do? Pulling out the edge pieces is usually the best bet in this situation. There are fewer of them, which makes going though them to test how similarly colored and designed pieces fit together easier. After you have the outer edge in place, the next step is sorting the pieces by similarities to test how they fit together. Although it is difficult at first, each piece you match brings into focus the direction you are headed.

Putting together a complicated jigsaw puzzle of this sort is similar to weaving the tapestry of your life. By first sorting out the straight-edged pieces, you are creating the defining edge, your moral and ethical beliefs, your personality, and your attitude—within which your tapestry will flourish. And, by looking for elements similar to your edge, you will be choosing those you are comfortable fitting into your tapestry. Although you might not have a clear vision of the direction in which you are going, each new thread you add to your life's tapestry will bring your path into focus.

"The journey of a thousand miles begins with one step."
—Lao-Tse

THE PUBLISHER

GENE ROBB FOCUSED my direction in life. As publisher of the Albany *Times Union*, he was a gentle, but leathery tough presence. Integrity shone from him. He had an energy engine driving him to seek the very best in all he devoted himself to. More importantly, he had the ability to encourage others to seek the best in themselves.

When I first had the opportunity to meet him, I was a young ad salesman supporting a new family and was going to school nights to further my education. Nothing glamorous, at least not to me. Gene, however, saw more. He plucked me from the many employee colleagues to train to be his successor, thus taking my tapestry in yet another new direction. The unique benefit of being at his side through a series of executive appointments and receiving his private tutelage—was deep, insightful, always value driven—a complete sharing of the motivations of his position, as contrasted to any unusual use of the power of it. "Talent," he would say with force and steady refrain, "is the essence of every great business." He urged that anyone privileged to influence the destiny of a business must be devoted to celebrate the talent of that place.

Gene sought out and saluted the goodness of character and talent. I never heard him raise his voice or utter a profanity. He wove the thread in me that changed the pattern of my tapestry; he offered the special fiber always to celebrate the talent of our business. I would often sit in front of his desk as he wove together all the intimate details necessary to an informed editorial, punctuating that commentary with advocacy never to forget the privilege of speaking to our marketplace through it. Character, success, celebrations of your associates—these comprised his lesson plan for me. Gene was a powerful thread so central to my own tapestry. His always-spiritual balance and refined demeanor often seemed a testimony to a larger force using his facility to excel for a greater good. Gene Robb was an angelic force for my tapestry. Then and now.

THE GREAT THING ABOUT LIFE is that there are no complicated maps to try to follow; you never have to worry about missing an exit or making a wrong turn because guarateed, if you keep yourself open to new experiences, you will always be on the right track. Sure, you might pull out a map during a cross-country vacation or even get on the Internet to figure the best way to avoid driving through New York City during rush-hour, but in your actual life—your family, your education, your work—is uncharted territory. And, although the individual decisions we make on the routes we travel will vary, it is important to see the twists and turns as being what makes life exciting. The key is not to force new directions into one's life.

Sometimes, the direction you are going in may seem wrong. It is full of so many bumps and potholes you wonder if you will survive. And during all that is going on, you may question how this could have occurred, stating over and over that what is taking place isn't something that should be happening to you.

When my daughter Marsha was five-years-old, she was diagnosed with cancer, and our family took off down an unpaved road in a very new direction. By sticking together and accepting the support of friends, we all survived this particular journey. All its up and downs taught me how important it is to look for one's angels during these difficult trips, rather than trying to go it alone.

When Laura Stoeckle was diagnosed with leukemia, it would have been very easy for her family to avoid the angels reaching out to help them, instead spending time trying to figure out why this had happened. Thankfully, they found themselves welcoming an unexpected blessing.

AN UNEXPECTED BLESSING
BY JAN STOECKLE

TWO YEARS AGO, my daughter, Laura was diagnosed with Acute Mylogenous Leukemia. Laura spent five and a half months in Mott Children's Hospital in Ann Arbor, Michigan. It was a terrible time for our family, but we were very blessed beyond our wildest imaginations.

We have a very close family, for which we are eternally grateful. They were, and continue to be, a constant source of strength. But we found that we had support from every quarter. People we work for and with, and people from not only our church, but also churches all over the area, and even across the country, lifted Laura (and us) up in prayer and offered us financial support.

We met a wonderful woman in Ann Arbor named Jennifer Scott. Jennifer was raised near our home and her parents attended our church. When she heard why we were in Ann Arbor, she called me at the hospital to see if she could help. We had never met, and I was not accustomed to asking a perfect stranger for help. She persisted. "Can I just bring you some magazines to help you pass the time?" This sounded safe, so I agreed. During her visit she asked my sister if there was anything more she could do. Linda suggested that since Warren, my husband, would be at the hospital alone with Laura for a few days, it would be helpful if Jennifer brought up a sandwich—we didn't leave Laura alone long enough for a trip to the cafeteria. That is how it started. From that request came meals, not sandwiches—full three-course meals everyday for weeks on end. She told folks at her church, St. Luke's Lutheran Church in Ann Arbor, and soon there was a brigade of new friends bringing food every day.

They brought much more than food. They reminded us that our world was much bigger than the hospital room and that we were not alone in the struggle. Because Jennifer and Linda were wise enough to offer and accept help even when I insisted that it was unnecessary, we gained the spiritual and, once again, the financial support of an entire congregation. I cannot tell you how incredible it was to take Laura to church at St. Luke's after we were out of the hospital. Pastor Mike, who had been a regular visitor during our time in Ann Arbor, introduced her to a standing ovation.

Laura's primary care nurse was Jeannie MacPowers. She was our guide through the entire process, and especially those first weeks as we struggled to find our way in a very different world. She created opportunities for me to hold and rock Laura in spite of all the IV lines and paraphernalia. She also helped us care for Laura's sister, Jessie, understanding how alone siblings feel during such an ordeal. She told us what to expect and helped us deal with it. After 12 hour shifts she came to Laura's ICU room on another floor, and brought her mail and read to her, even though Laura was in a drug induced coma, on dialysis and a respirator.

When Laura was back on the oncology floor and doing better, Jeannie came back after her shift and stayed with Laura and Jessie so Warren and I could go out to dinner.

There were many others who just "did" for us. They made sure we knew we were cared for and it made all the difference. We are stronger and still together, largely as a result of this wonderful support.

The story is not over, but it does have a happy second chapter. Laura and Jessie are both honor-roll students, and Warren and I are both still working—after never missing a paycheck from either of our jobs during our long absence.

Each of us wakes up every day in the presence of miracles. My family and I are blessed with a second chance to be truly aware of them.

> *"What do we live for if it is not to make*
> *life less difficult for each other?"*
> –GEORGE ELIOT

HAVE YOU EVER FOUND yourself stuck in the middle, as if being pulled in so many directions you no longer had the ability to move forward or backward, much less side to side? Sometimes it is as simple as loosening a knotted thread in your tapestry when this happens. Sometimes, though, the best thing to do is to cut your ties so you can move again. Jessie Lair once said, "If you want something very, very badly, let it go free. If it comes back to you, it is yours forever. If it doesn't, it was never yours to begin with." In either of these situations, it is nice to have the benefit of another thread already weaving its way through your tapestry. More often than not, you will find the direction you are headed in requires a difficult design of multiple threads, one of which tends to have the insight of an angel.

A SIMPLE GROCER

HE ALWAYS DESCRIBED himself as a simple grocer. Indeed, when Frank J. Nigro rented his first compact corner grocery store on the corner of South Allen and Central Avenues in Albany, New York, this description seemed generous, since he sold only fruits and vegetables in the modest store. However, Frank creatively merchandised everything from each stalk of celery to each shining apple in outdoor bins that brimmed with impeccably positioned displays.

His dream was for his store, Albany Public Market, to one day be a full-fledged supermarket, where he could let his merchandising flair roam. It was not many years before he indeed managed a bank loan and opened a major full-service supermarket about one mile up the road from his first corner-stand store.

Within a few years, Frank opened several area super-markets and Albany Public Market became the dominant grocery chain in the entire area. It was at this point of business maturity that he became a thread of life in my ever-developing personal tapestry.

During that time in the Albany area's media history, the Gannett corporation-owned evening *Knickerbocker News* was the dominant advertising vehicle for several merchan-dise categories. This included the grocery ads, in which the paper enjoyed a 100 percent share of the field. There was no share in the morning *Times Union* where I worked.

At that time, I was a classified advertising salesman, only recently married and seeking a move to the display ad staff where the salary was higher. I proposed to our advertising director, Mark Collins, that he let me have a chance to handle the grocery advertising sales territory while I retained my classified ad job. No increase in salary, I proposed, unless I could produce results in a reasonable time. He agreed, and I became a new retail salesman handling the grocery accounts, with zero business.

I immersed myself in studying the grocery business and culling out small suggestions for any merchant to improve his business. The ads from the competing *Knickerbocker News* became my creative ammunition. I re-designed each ad, had it set in type and delivered proofs to every grocery business as an example of how they might improve their advertising.

While I called on every grocer each week, I called on Albany Public Markets and Frank Nigro every single day. He was an impeccable man—medium in height, with shining hair slicked straight back, and a classic Italian face, including a Roman nose any sculptor would be proud of.

Within two months, Frank Nigro called me aside, stared directly at me, hunched his shoulder, and announced that starting the next week he would be splitting his ten ad pages and giving five of those to the *Times Union*. Celebration! Because his stores were the food category leaders, all the other grocery stores followed his lead within a few weeks and suddenly my *Times Union* had 55 percent of the grocery advertising.

Because I continued to call on Frank every day with some new idea, we became very close. Within a few years there came an opportunity for me to apply for the retail advertising manager position at the newspaper. When I applied, I was told I was too young and would not be considered. Disappointed, I set off for my daily call on Frank Nigro. Because he knew me so well, he could sense my slump and asked what was wrong. I explained that I had been turned down for the manager slot as being too young.

"Not a problem," said Frank, "just go down today and quit." I told him I had a family to support and could not simply quit my job. He said, "You will not be out of a job. You will come to Albany Public Markets on Monday and become my advertising and promotion manager." I did just that.

Some six weeks later I received an invitation to lunch from the ad director of the *Times Union*, and then I went for the first time as a customer rather than a salesman. During lunch, the director, Roger Coryell, told me he had re-assessed my credentials and concluded that, although I was young, I was the right man for the retail ad manager position. I listened with my heart wildly beating, but gave no response except to listen. After lunch, I went into Frank Nigro's office. He looked up from his paperwork with a slight smile and said, "They offered you the job, didn't they?" I told him they had, but I did not comment since I was now working for him. "Your destiny is to be in the newspaper business, not the grocery business. All I did in providing you this job was to offer you a port in the storm until the newspaper executives came to their senses."

A port in the storm; that phrase never left me as I returned to the newspaper and began a journey that would ultimately take me to the helm of our company for twenty years.

Frank J. Nigro, called FJN by friends and associates, proved to be a major thread in my life tapestry. He was a guide, an advocate, and an instrument who shaped my destiny. I am very comfortable with the notion that he may well have been a ready vehicle for a spirit force I never saw, but only sensed, when I first began my daily visits to him. All the grocery storeowners were available for that daily call, but it was he who became my daily target. And as time would prove, he also became the vendor offering advice to strengthen my commitment, which was to be a source of guidance for others who would cross my path. I became his customer, and he, another angel thread in my strengthening tapestry.

TRAINING WHEELS; most of us learned how to ride a bike by first relying on training wheels. These "trainers" saved us from a few extra skinned knees and hands by giving us the support we needed until we were able to balance ourselves.

When FJN offered me a "port in the storm," he offered me an opportunity to try my hand at doing something new. In doing so, he gifted me with the chance to learn how to balance myself without the aid of my training wheels. This was while he still supported me as I learned how to start and stop without the aid of the curb or my already skinned knees. This quality of sticking by and helping others was just one of the many common threads shared with me during my research of angels.

New Levels
by Bob Carlquist

EVERYONE HAS A DIFFERENT notion of angels. My notion of angels involves people who have appeared in my life at just the right moment and have touched my life in very special ways. The impact of those encounters has changed my life forever and for the better.

One such encounter for me occurred in 1998. As part of that year's American Leadership Forum class in Houston, a diverse group of twenty-four community, civic and business leaders was brought together to study leadership. Its purpose was to apply the skills learned from working together on this project to building a better and stronger community for everyone.

Our class traveled to a mountain camp on an outward-bound program designed to teach valuable skills in building organizations and a stronger community. It was intended to help the group bond and build a cohesiveness that would enable us to work together and more effectively deal with our own differences. The entire experience had a profound effect on me. But it was the rock climbing experience that made me think of angels.

On Saturday night, we were briefed about the planned Sunday morning hike to a mountain some distance away, which we would climb. We were told about the equipment we would be using and backpacking with us. Several of us had not understood that climbing up the face of a mountain would be part of our experience. The notion of a vertical climb up the sheer face of a granite rock mountain began to sink in as the guides spoke. We were just getting to know each other. Were we to depend on people we barely knew?

Early Sunday morning, after breakfast, our group began the march to the mountain we would climb. We were told how to find footholds and handholds in the granite in order to pull ourselves up the mountain. We were also taught how to use the safety lines and equipment that we were being provided. One end of a rope was to be tied to a harness on the climber. The other end was to be held and managed by someone way above the climber on the mountain.

We practiced again and again. We wanted to make certain that everyone had learned the proper technique for handling the safety rope. We slid into our harnesses and cinched them so that we did not have to do this at the base of the mountain. We began walking up the leg of the trail to the face. The trail became rockier and steeper as we came closer to our destination.

We all stood looking up at what we were about to climb. Five ropes had been dropped from sixty feet above. To an experienced climber this was a small step. For us it loomed as a "giant leap for mankind."

A few of our classmates quickly volunteered to climb to the top of the face and hold the ropes for climbers. Those of us below reached out and touched the rock as if we were trying to make friends with it.

It was a slow process making it up the face. In the midst of my struggle, friends and classmates below began cheering me on. Their enthusiastic voices lifted me. They encouraged me. They cared whether I made it. I was not alone.

I struggled for the final twenty feet. I needed only a ledge to make it over to the next one. I also needed the little strength that remained in the muscles in my arms and legs to make it over this final obstacle. Almost there. The climb had been relatively fast up to this point. Now everything seemed too slow. I desperately wanted to hurry and cross the finish line. The rope remained taut. I made a lunge and grasped a rock just over the upper side of the ledge still invisible to me. With one quick motion, I pulled myself over the top. As I went up, I came face to face with the person who had been holding the rope for me. He and the others let out a loud cheer. They made me feel as if I had just won a major Olympic event. As I relaxed, Larry Hall held my rope tight. He grinned at me with the biggest Cheshire cat expression I had ever seen in my life. I will never forget his smile and look of encouragement. They were uplifting. It was as if a guardian angel was smiling down on me.

The symbolism of the moment will stay with me and lift me the rest of my life. The climb that we make throughout our life is often difficult. Many times, it is slow and tedious, and filled with obstacles and setbacks. Some try to prove they can make it on their own. It cannot be done alone. We are helped bfy angels who are there to get us started. We are cheered and encouraged by angels along the way, often when the going gets particularly tough. We just have to listen and feel their presence, to take a moment to savor the majesty of everything around us. And I am always reminded that there is an angel holding the rope for us, trying to keep us safe. The angel can be a husband or wife, a parent or other relative, or a friend for life like Larry Hall.

Spiritual Oasis

ANGELS AS SPIRITUAL GUIDES
BY DAVID SAN FILIPPO, PH.D.

The existence of angels has been discussed for centuries in legendary, philosophical and religious writings. Angels are perceived to be superhuman entities which exist to be servants of a higher being. These spiritual beings are thought to be intermediaries between God and human kind. They are believed to perform the tasks of messengers, guides and guardians. Many people have reported encounters with beings of light or angelic forms recognizable to the beholder.

In a modern encounter with a "comforting angel," a woman who was severely injured in an automobile accident reported that she was "comforted" by an angel who came in the form of a man surrounded by a pink glow. His movements were graceful and fluid. His hands were extended, almost reassuringly, palm open to her. He had the most loving eyes she had ever seen and the kindest smile.

In the Judeo-Christain and Islamic religions, angels are believed to act as spiritual guides in the believer's life. The philosopher Thomas Aquinas believed that angels are 100 percent spirits that have no mass or matter and take up no space. He equated their existence to human thought.

Through the psychic phenomenon or near-death experiences, individuals have seen angels and experienced their comfort, protection and love. Angels appear to have an important part as guides.

They act as messengers to warn the near-death experiencer to remember what he has undergone and to strive to abstain from any former inappropriate behavior. Individuals obtain the understanding that spiritually concerns the ability to love other people, not merely specific doctrines and denominations, and that the importance of human life is service to others and the seeking of knowledge.

Angels do exist, not necessarily in the images that artists and sculptors have portrayed them, or in the personages that writers have depicted them. They exist in the essence of their angelic behaviors.

Change

⤜⤛

"Mountains viewed from a distance seem unscalable,
but they can be climbed, and the way to begin is to
take the first upward step. From that moment
the mountains are less high. The slopes
seem to level off as we near them."
—ANONYMOUS

A friend of mine tells a story of how she and her mother used to make the most beautiful quilts together. She would sew the top on the machine, and her mother, who did not believe in sewing with machines, hand-stitched the underside. As my friend tells the story, this is how she and her mother went about doing these quilts for years—one not having the patience to deal with the old way of doing things and the other not willing to change to a new way. When her mother passed, my friend was faced with doing the underside of the quilt. For the first time, she hand-stitched the underside and also for the first time, had an appreciation for her mother's way—a way she wished she had appreciated earlier.

"How many angels are there?
One who transforms our life is plenty."
—ANONYMOUS

ROOM 401

CREAM COLORED WALLS with a single divider curtain between them were the basic décor of this one of many intensive cardiac care hospital rooms. Each room was exactly alike; only the distinction of patients sharing the two-in-one bedroom expressed the difference.

My behind-the-curtain roommate was a glint-in-the-eye, mischievous, gargling-humor-through-the-tubes-in-his-throat, pixie-like chap named Gene Wald. We shared the room and the triggering circumstances of severe heart attacks.

With all the uncertainty, confusion, and discomfort of a debilitating heart problem, anyone could experience a permanent downswing in mood, unless his or her room-mate was someone like Gene Wald.

Gene's approach to the 32 days we shared room 401 was to focus on the fun. Our room became the hub for our wing of the hospital's ambulatory patients, nurses, and off-duty doctors, to congregate for food, good company and good will. "Tubes up" as he was, Gene managed to be the magnet for all, the spark to ignite that goodwill. And, he taught me to join in the spirit of the moment.

Some several years before my heart attack, my family and I moved from our upstate New York hometown to our

New Jersey home, which offered easy commuter access to my office in New York City and the Newark airport. With that move, we left behind all of our life-long friends and business associates. Now, traveling the country overseeing our nationwide group of newspaper companies, I was simply too busy to notice that I had not developed new pals; my life had become entirely focused on my work and my family.

Gene became my first new friend during that month plus in the hospital. Our meeting was purely due to each of us having a heart attack, going to the same hospital and randomly being assigned to share the same room. Room 401, my roommate, and the atmosphere of goodwill in the face of adversity were a launching pad for a changed life. Room 401 proved to be the incubator preparing me to begin a new life phase with an abundance of friends, a focus on my physical well-being, and a more balanced attitude about the pressures of business.

Gene graduated from 401 first. I went on to the New York Hospital for open-heart surgery and was told I would need several months of quiet rest before I could expect to take even the smallest baby steps towards a normal life. I could not drive a car. I could not walk more than a block. I could only sit and hope my body would mend.

On my first day home, Gene arrived and asked me to join him in building a model airplane. The next day he came with a heart happy picnic from a local deli, and the next day he took me for a ride in the country. In fact, since he was also mending from a less severe heart condition, but had not yet been released to return to his work, he came to see me with some fresh activity every single day for six weeks.

In the seventh week, with my vigor returning, he drove me to his local exercise club where he had gifted me a trial membership. In the eighth week, with my daily walks now at three miles a day, Gene had me join his Saturday walking group for their weekly jaunt.

A few years later, with our friendship robust, Gene's heart again suffered from an attack. Sadly, he did not survive. Although his body closed down, his sparkling spirit did not. Gene's "live life with a smile" attitude and caring way live on in the lives of all those he touched. Because Gene introduced me to the hum of the good humor, which proved to be the centerpiece of my health club and Saturday walking friends, my life has never returned to the imbalance of earlier days.

Room 401, with cream colored walls and a single room divider was different from any other room in the cardiac unit. The difference was the joy filled spirit of Gene Wald, who chose me to be the happy recipient of his guidance and support. The threads of Gene are front and center, brilliant elements in my tapestry. Often one's middle years have light patterns already woven. Because of Gene, I found the middle age slice of life so enriched by the buoyant qualities of change infused into my tapestry. He was an angel thread for me.

CHANGE IS INTERESTING. Although it is one of the contants of life, it is completely unpredictable. Sometimes it arrives when we are expecting it. Other times it shows up completely unannounced like an uninvited guest, allowing us no time to prepare for the alterations we will have to make in our lives.

When we invite change, we usually have a wonderful time with it. We announce its arrival to others and revel in the freshness of it. We enjoy it. But, when it descends upon us without an invite, we are forced to find a way to fit it into our busy schedule. Although doing this may seem like an impossible juggling act, it is important to view change as a challenge and not as a problem.

When I first had my heart attack, I could not imagine it as anything other than a problem. Now, though, I recall it as the challenge I had to face in order to experience the well-needed life transformation by angelic Gene Wald.

CHALLENGES–
ONLY CHALLENGES
BY TIM KELLY

IN 1978, I had a position as an intern with the now defunct/ renamed/reinvented Department of Health, Education and Welfare. This was during the summer between my graduation from high school and my entry into the University of Maryland at College Park. I was assigned to the Division of Emergency Medical Services in Hyattsville, Maryland, as a technical writer. As I recall, DEMS's primary responsibilities were making grants to fledgling and rural EMS operations and educating people about the role of EMS in their communities.

My boss was the deputy director of the division, a fiery Irishman named John D. Reardon. Mr. Reardon was in his 50's, tall, bald-headed and graying, and friendly, with a wit like a whip and a smile like a salesman. He ran the division's day-to-day operations in the absence of the director, an M.D. who seemed never to be there. He took his mission seriously, but never himself or the bureaucracy.

Mr. Reardon and I talked quite a bit that summer. Looking back on it now, from the perspective of a boss, it was a remarkable amount of time. He showed me how government agencies tried to work and how the people who ran them tried to work around them. He mentored me back before they had a name for it, and in his easy role of philosopher-civil servant, he offered me practical advice that I did not fully appreciate until much later.

I think of him now because of something he repeated to me several times that summer of '78. On one level, it is another clever little bromide. On another level, it is a philosophy I found easy to embrace and have employed ever since. I remember the morning I barged into his office (the first of many times) to announce, "Mr. Reardon, we have a problem." He looked up from his work, shoved his cheaters down his nose and, effecting an easy brogue, said, "Timothy, me boy, there are no problems, only challenges."

Maybe somebody had said that before, maybe not. It might seem glib today, but I assure you, nothing at that point in my life had ever sounded more profound. I am not sure I ever properly said goodbye to Mr. Reardon, but I think of him every time someone tells me we have a problem.

"Vision is the art of seeing things invisible."
— JONATHON SWIFT

CHANGE IS NOT BAD; it is more often than not opportunity in disguise. When I had my heart attack, I was not thrilled with the prospect of going into surgery, but that heart attack led me to one of the dearest friends I have ever had. And even earlier in life, when I unintentionally dropped the mattress on my foreman, the thud it created definitely did not sound like opportunity knocking or feel like a challenge. It was a problem.

As with all things in life, as I gained experience I soon saw unexpected and initially unwanted change to have a dimension of higher purpose in store for my tapestry. Change became the tool by which I learned to introduce new patterns into my life. Norman Vincent Peale actually explained this better when he used it as an example in the following story:

Many of the world's finest oriental rugs come from little villages in the Middle East. Each rug is hand-produced by a crew of men and boys under the direction of a master weaver.

Since ordinarily they work from the underside of the rug-to-be, it frequently happens that a weaver absent-mindedly makes a mistake and introduces a color that is not according to the pattern. When this occurs, the master weaver, instead of having the work pulled out in order to correct the color sequence, will find some way to incorporate the mistake harmoniously into the overall pattern.

Imagine yourself to be the master weaver. What might feel like a mistake is really an opportunity that change has presented to you to introduce previously unconsidered patterns to your tapestry.

Sara's Song

His name was first mentioned to me by Dr. Rob Gilbert, a local university professor. I had just addressed his graduate class in sports psychology when Dr. Gilbert told me that Rich Ruffalo had spoken to his class the month before, and he believed Rich and I would enjoy knowing each other.

After a few failed stabs at phone tag, I finally made contact with Rich and made a date to visit him. When I arrived at his handsome split ranch home, I rang the doorbell with a sense of excitement. As the door opened, I extended my hand in greeting. Standing before me was this giant of a man, well over six and a half feet tall, looking like the interior line of a pro-football team. Rather than shake my hand, he said, "Come here. I want to hug you!" He literally picked me up and I hung from his embrace, legs dangling like a Raggedy Andy doll. A passerby would have thought the two of us looked like a still photo embraced by the rectangular frame of the door.

Once he gently set me back on my feet, Rich asked that I follow him to his porch where we would chat. He walked in front of me, settled into a chaise lounge and suggested I sit in the lawn chair next to him. Just as I began to more formally introduce myself, his six-year-old daughter, Sara, came bouncing onto the porch. She settled into her father's lap and asked whether they could sing their special song before she said "night-night." Rich pulled her up close to his cheek and Sara turned her sweet face to me, the guest audience, and beamed her radiant smile. Rich's baritone joined with her lovely soprano and they sang aloud, *We Have Come to Teach*. Four verses. In perfect harmony. Sara, wearing her pastel yellow Winnie-the-Pooh nightgownand the content look of a loved child, nestled right up to her daddy's cheek. With the song concluded, Sara kissed us both and toddled off to sleep.

"I am a teacher," Rich said to me. He explained that he taught biology in a local high school and had been honored by the Disney Corporation as the nationwide teacher of the year. The song, he said, was the theme music for the event, and Sara had loved it so much that it had become their personal tradition for their evening goodnights.

Rich then turned his face toward me and asked, "Have you noticed I have not been looking at you?" I replied that I did, but thought that I had not yet said anything to compel his interest.

He drew a deep breath and told me he had not looked at me because he could not see me. He was blind. His sight, he said, had left him four years after college. As his sight dimmed, he said, it was replaced with a deep bitterness. Why me? That became the question that would not leave his mind.

With his teaching career threatened, only the participation in athletic events for the blind gave him any sense of relief and wholeness. He did continue to teach with the aid of a sighted proctor. Because he needed to raise the funds to pay for his travel to the athletic competitions, he would contact local organizations to sponsor him and repay them by speaking to their employees about his experiences. Quite unintentionally, he found himself in demand as a speaker for a growing number of local groups. Audience members moved by his comments encouraged him to become a professional speaker, as did his caring wife, Diane. Although he started quite tentatively, Rich soon found himself in high demand as a polished and highly impactful professional speaker.

The trigger event, he told me, was his realization that he had a gift to share. It occurred at a St. Louis track event when he felt a tug on his sleeve, accompanied by a woman's voice telling him she was there with 31 children from the St. Louis School for the Blind. They had come, she said, to "touch you today." Rich said he knelt down and each child rubbed his muscular arm, shoulder and neck. When he stood to throw the javelin, he could hear the children cheering. Their voices gave him momentum, and that day he threw the javelin further than he ever had before. More important than the gold medal he won, he said, was the vision he saw as the javelin left his hand; he was blind because others needed him to inspire them to choose to see the light of possibility rather than grim dim despair.

Once triggered, his speaking career soared. The Disney honor came, and his life became one of illumination for others. I mentioned my own beginning aspirations to become a speaker sharing insights with others. We finished the evening with another warm hug and I left him, sensing I had tapped into a new friendship and an inspiration.

A few weeks later, Rich called me and said Sara had loved singing her song for an audience. She wanted to thank me for listening and ask for a repeat performance. With that said, Rich put his darling Sara on and she said, "*We Have Come to Teach* is my favorite song, and I want to sing it again for you with daddy." And over the telephone, I again felt the joy effected by hearing the sweet duet.

Rich then said he had another reason for calling. He wanted to introduce me to Nancy Vogl, owner of The Universal Speakers Bureau. "She was," he said, "a woman with a special spirit."

Rich dialed Nancy's phone with me still on the wire and introduced us to each other as "people with a special spirit." He told her I was his daughter Sara's most favorite recent audience, who also needed speaking guidance from a pro. Nancy and I chatted a bit, and she said she would like to hear me speak at an event. After that, she explained, she would consider working with me to guide me toward a presence in the speaking world.

Later that week I caught up with Rich to thank him. He told me that after I had left our first meeting on his porch, he went in to kiss his Sara goodnight again. She whispered to him, "Daddy, our song says we have come to teach, and your new friend Bob came here to tell us 'I have come to listen.' You should teach him Daddy."

Teach me Rich had. In fact, he opened a new door to the speaking world for me, all because he had the insight to see through a seemingly dismal black situation and pass what he learned to me through his six-year-old angel singing her favorite song.

BLACK HAS ALWAYS BEEN my least favorite color. I like Carolina blue, Van Gogh yellow, and ruby red. I prefer bright, vibrant, smile-introducing colors. And even though I've always been told that black is the sum of all the primary colors added together, I've never associated anything other than gloom and doom with it—until now.

As various angel threads were shared with me, I realized how easy it could be to associate black with certain changes that occur, instead of trying to see all the brilliant colors muddled together. Edy Nathan, who is a grief therapist, was one of the first threads encouraging me to change my opinion of black by describing her experience of seeing the angelic golden threads intertwined with the death of her soulmate, which also outlined a glorious new purpose for her life.

THE SHAPE OF HOPE
BY EDY NATHAN

WHEN I WAS 24 YEARS OLD, I met Paul, a man who was my soulmate and who was 25 years older than I am. When our eyes met across a truly crowded room, there was an instant attraction, a sense that somehow we had finally found each other and that it had been a long search.

I was in school getting a master's degree that would enable me to go into the corporate world, to train employees and employers to cope with the onslaught of drugs in the workplace. Creating a dynamic approach for the corporate arena, I was excited about that potential in this career.

About a year into the program, Paul, who was an actor and traveled extensively with his career, came back home feeling ill. After convincing him that he had to go to the hospital, he helplessly relented. Before I knew it, we were deluged with doctors' reports, none of which were in English. After deciphering the medical mumbo jumbo, it seemed apparent that cancer had spread to his lungs and that the only hope was a lung dissection. Reluctantly, we agreed to this and much more, though at the time we did not know it. Because Paul had little money, we were stuck at the beck and call of the physicians at the local veterans' hospital. Though the care was sufficient, we had to be on our toes for even the essential things. I found myself living at the hospital day and night. I would go to school, work my job as a bartender, and then go to the hospital. I would often sleep in his four-bedded room throughout the night.

The surgery went well; he made it through. The pain was so excruciating and his ability to cope with life in a hopeful manner was also diminishing. I felt ill-equipped to handle what this man, this human being, was going through. He, who was my best friend, my lover, my confidant and the holder of my secrets, was losing ground because he could not handle the betrayal of his body.

I am a go-getter. I try to create success wherever I go. I do not, under any circumstance, know what to do with helplessness except to try to conquer it. Thus began my departure from the world of drugs and corporate training. I got every book I could on cancer, illness, death, grief and loss. It was apparent to me and to Paul that we were riding a wave that would certainly end up in catastrophe.

We knew that the cancer had a voice of its own and that the voice felt loud and angry and doomed. We knew we had to get out of this space and find some way to escape from the mire of doom that left us mute. How do you find a voice in light of the fact that everything around you feels like it is dying? This question we asked ourselves and continued to process throughout his life and our life together.

There is power in knowledge. Therefore, we educated ourselves about his form of cancer. We talked to doctors, we annoyed them, and we did not let them forget that we were human beings, and not just social security numbers to be registered for the living and the dead. The doctors began to talk with us. The nurses helped us out and we felt just the tiniest bit of life within our surroundings. We took the reality of this illness to propel us to new dimensions.

I realized then that I had good therapeutic skills and knew that if anyone was going to help us get through this, I was going to have to be that person. My mission was to help myself and Paul through the dying process.

With reasonable expectations, we entered into a journey that allowed us to grieve together, cry together, laugh together and find hope together. Hope takes on many different forms when dealing with dying. It can be delivered through an honest communication, can be held onto because there is a great love that is being shared, and can be fostered through empowerment attained through the choices one makes about how he or she wants to die.

It is because we realized we had power that Paul and I were able to live through, grieve through and rejoice through his dying process. We focused on how we could be proactive. We began to learn that we did have choices. Instead of letting his hair fall out, we decided to shave his head ourselves.

What Paul's death did to me was to change my life forever. I could not think about returning to the life I had begun, and I needed to entertain a different life that would entail helping people cope with their grief. I started groups for people who were grieving. I spoke at universities and colleges on the topic of death and dying, and on strategies to make it easier for all the survivors.

I started a private practice, and my entire life focus changed. I had become more independent, confident and self-assured. What I had to say and to offer could have some importance to others. His death allowed me to grow-up and become the very person I am today. His death was a gift to me. It allowed me to develop into a grief therapist who reaches out to hundreds of people a year. His voice, his pain and his love are the very seed of what has blossomed into the work I do on a daily basis. In a way he did not die, he just took on a different form that reaches out through my voice. He is my angel.

FLOWERS GROW OUT OF DARK MOMENTS
BY CORITA KENT

HAVE YOU EVER NOTICED a flower growing out of a crack in the sidewalk? Although it is very rare that I see one, when I do, I always stop to consider the small feat this flower has accomplished. It cannot be easy living in a literal stomping ground.

Clare Boothe Luce once said, "Courage is the ladder on which all other virtues mount." I believe that if there is one reason why something as small as a flower in a crack in a sidewalk can adapt to the world treading around, it is because of courage.

SPEAKER/AUTHOR RAINBOW

SPORTS PSYCHOLOGY, taught by Dr. Rob Gilbert (the teacher who introduced me to Rich Ruffalo), was a graduate degree class I showed up at to do a guest lecture. The give and take of the class following the formal remarks resulted in an energetic and satisfying evening. After the students left, Dr. Rob asked me to sit with him for a bit so he could know me better. During the course of our chat, he told me that while teaching was his every day assignment, his passion was the entire subject of public speaking.

Over a Diet Coke, Dr. Rob told me his own compelling personal story. In graduate school, he found himself introduced to a professor who specialized in programs for speaking excellence. Dr. Rob asked if he could be a student and was told that he would be accepted only if he gave himself over completely to the instructive guidance. He agreed and was told that he should have confidence that he would be able to stand before a class and give a mesmerizing speech before the semester's end. Rob felt this was a challenging dream, but committed himself to full acceptance of the teacher's methodology.

Leaning over his desk to emphasize the point during our chat, he told me that when the day came that he did indeed deliver his first-ever speech, he felt as if he was living the first day of his life. The joy he felt encouraged him to complete his Ph.D. and specialize in providing speaker guidance to every student who crossed his path.

He told me that he collected the audio tapes of many great speakers and, now learning of my own beginning interest in becoming a professional speaker, he would put together a collection of his favorite speaker tapes for me to hear. When next we met for a Saturday lunch, he delivered me the complete tapes of Bishop Fulton J. Sheen, tapes of the philosopher/author/speaker Og Mandino, and a collection of insights on change from his own personal favorite, Dr. Richard Byrnes.

They all became my constant companions; in the car while driving; in my walkman while hiking; as background when reading at home. Rob had suggested that I listen for authenticity, the pauses, and the range of feelings these great speakers all shared. Listen I did for months while the gifts of those memorable speakers were woven into my psyche.

Combined with the encouragement of my friend, speaker/teacher Rich Ruffalo, I found myself increasingly attracted to the rare privilege a speaker has to stand alone before an audience and, just possibly, be the instrument encouraging life insight, a life change, a transformation in some unknown audience member. The prospect was delicious.

As CHILDREN, WE LEARN from others how to deal with change and how to distribute our emotions accordingly—feel happy and smile during births and holidays, and feel sad and cry during funerals. There are, however, some changes that no one can prepare us for—those "it will never happen to me or someone I know" changes. And when they happen, the world seems to crash down around us because everything we thought we knew—thought we could handle—seems to fade away, and we have to find ourselves again through all the unleashed emotions we've experienced and never knew existed.

There is no one way to pull out of these times, no key, no map. However, by choosing to lean on the support of the threads in our tapestry, we can use their strength to buttress ourselves. Although such times are the ultimate test of its strength, it is important not to focus on the why. There are certain things that happen for which there is no answer.

SHE GAVE ME LIFE
BY AMANDA

ON MAY 5TH, 1995, my friend Melissa and I went out to dinner. We belonged to the same sorority at school and had been friendly from the time I pledged. Melissa was a year older than I was and was going to graduate from our school two weeks later. Just weeks before this particular dinner date, we discovered that our grandparents, who all lived in Florida, were best friends. We laughed over the bond we shared.

As we sat over dinner, Melissa described her on-going job search. She was so panicked that she would be unable to find a job, and I remember reminding her that her parents would not throw her out if she was jobless at graduation. Later, this conversation would make me think that she was so worried because the path of her life was so unclear and unplanned.

When we finished dinner, we left the restaurant and got into my car. As I was about to close my door, a man grabbed it and showed a gun by his side. I begged him just to take the car, but my weak pleas were to no avail. He ordered me out of the car, and I then realized that there was another man at Melissa's side keeping her from closing the door.

We were both forced into the back seat of the car and the two men entered the front. The driver immediately took off as the passenger kept a gun in our faces.

Melissa more forcefully told the men to take the car and to let us go, and was answered by being shot. The moment the passenger shot her, her head fell in my lap. The passenger asked me if I was going to cooperate and I shook my head. He immediately told me to give him my jewelry and to take Melissa's off. I remember that she moved slightly to make this easier for me.

The men pulled off the highway and into a very dangerous neighborhood. After driving around for a few minutes, the driver stopped the car near a park. Both men got out of the car and Melissa whispered my name. I was too terrified to say anything, but I wish I had had the courage to comfort her in some way with my voice.

The men opened the door and pulled Melissa out by her legs. They shut the door and I heard one shot. The passenger then got in the back seat of the car and raped me.

Several minutes later, the driver stopped the car in a pitch-black alley. I was ordered out of the car. I walked away from the car and looked back. At that moment, I was shot in the face three times. I dropped to the ground, instinctively knowing to play dead. I heard the car drive off as I lay on the ground. I felt certain that I was going to die and so I decided just to close my eyes and go to sleep.

After a few seconds, I tried to move. I quickly realized that my body was fine, although there was blood everywhere, and that I could get up. I ran to a run-down house with tons of cars outside it. I banged on the door and the people inside refused to help me because they had no phone.

After I kept banging, one man came out of the house and said he would get help for me. He told me to wait outside his house. I did not want to wait so I kept running down this dark street. I had blood all over me and could not see out of my left eye. I remember thinking to myself that I was in the most dangerous area in the state, but knew that nothing else could possibly happen to me.

I kept running without even feeling out of breath. Eventually I came upon two people getting out of their driveway. I asked them to help me and told them I had been shot. They did not respond to me, and I started running again. Within a few seconds, the man drove up behind me. I got in his car and was screaming hysterically. He kept moving his arm trying to calm me down. I realized that he could not speak and that is why he did not answer me when I asked for help. I later discovered that he had throat cancer.

This man brought me to the police station in town and soon I was in an ambulance on my way to a hospital. I told the police that Melissa was in a park somewhere and that she was probably alive.

In the ambulance, I kept thinking that if I could just close my eyes I would die and be out of pain. The ambulance attendant kept talking to me and telling me that I had to stay awake. I remember being extremely annoyed that he kept talking to me, but I now realize he was just trying to make me believe that I was fine.

The details from here are not important, except that I learned that Melissa had died. I guess I knew all along but I really believed that she was able to run and find help as well. When I learned that she had died soon after the second shot, I knew that she was responsible for keeping me alive. Somehow, she was able to protect me and bring the man who saved me. How else could I explain this gentle stranger who helped me when there was no one else who could?

I am almost the person that I was before this incident, in some ways better. The doctors considered it a miracle that I lived. It is as if the bullets in my head were drawn from anywhere that they could have done harm.

"Each of us has a guardian angel."

Spiritual Oasis

FROM FEAR TO GRACE
BY LO ANNE MAYER, ANGEL HEALER

Coming to the Earth is a soul's decision, based upon God's consent and directive, and the soul's desire to learn specific lessons. I have also come to understand that each of our souls is given a guardian angel at conception to help us throughout life and to bring us back home to God when we are finished with our physical body.

As I arrived on Earth in 1941, the winds of World War II polluted the thoughts and conversations of those helping me struggle to be born. Fear was everywhere: on the airbase where my military parents lived; in the South that housed those airbases, where blacks and white feared each other; in all the newspapers, radios and movies that focused on the worldwide fear of war. In that environment it was easy to forget the love of God and the lessons my soul agreed to learn, as well as the mission I agreed to carry out. Thank heaven my guardian angel would not let me forget!

I believe that I came to Earth to overcome fear, to learn patience and to teach healing love. Being born in the midst of wartime was a perfect environment for my soul's lessons.

God and I planned well! Gently and progressively, I was introduced to the difference between fear and love: the gentle love of my mother's caresses which calmed the bodily fears of my asthma and pneumonia; the kind and loving words of a priest who healed my nightmares of the hell, fire and brimstone religion that was my family's choice; the safety of my cousin's love as we talked about about my fears concerning my parents' divorce; the kindness of a classmate as I fearfully entered my fifth school in nine years; the love of my husband as I faced the fear of pregnancy for the first time and the arrival of our six children, with all the hopes, fears and challenges that parenting brings. Love for my family inspired me to learn many healing techniques to help face and overcome fear.

As I followed my life's path, my guardian angel introduced me to people, places, ideas, and insights, which led me to transform the fear of living into the love of healing. Through many Divine Appointments, I was introduced to all kinds of healing techniques, such as therapeutic touch, nutrition, charismatic prayer, metaphysics, Reiki, mind-body healing, and angelic mediation. Each lesson was carefully orchestrated for use in my personal life and to add to my education. For 25 years I studied and earned my Ph.D. in patience!

Gradually, with my angel's help, I remembered my soul's mission. Finally I understood that the healing I had learned for the benefit of my family could be shared with others. And so it evolved into opportunities to teach and share healing with people outside of my family. It is no accident that these opportunities came exactly at the time when many people are looking for ways to empower themselves with healing.

The worldwide fear is not much different than it was in 1941. Healing is still needed all over the planet. I look at my grandchildren and recommit to sharing my understanding of healing. No child should be born into fear, but they are every day!

The awareness of the angels around the globe is an ecumenical reminder that God still gives humans the grace and the opportunities to love one another. The choice is clear: Fear versus Love. My guardian angel tells me that I have the opportunity to share peace, love and healing every day. My life experience has taught me that angels light the way from Fear to Grace. All I have to do is follow the light of the angels. I plan to do so. Do you want to come?

"… he allowed himself to be swayed by his conviction that
human beings are not born once and for all on the day
their mothers give birth to them, but that life obliges
them over again to give birth to themselves."
— GABRIEL GARCIA MARQUEZ

The Trimmings

"Do more than exist – live.
Do more than touch – feel.
Do more than look – observe.
Do more than read – absorb.
Do more than hear – listen.
Do more than listen – understand"
–JOHN H. RHODES

After retiring from being with the Hearst Corporation for over forty years and beginning a new career as a motivational speaker, the statement I seem to hear on a daily basis is: "I thought you retired."

It seems that there is a notion that when one retires, he or she is expected to move to a specialized community in Florida to spend the rest of life playing golf. I have nothing against golf, and I do love my family vacations in Florida, but when I left the Hearst Corporation I regarded retirement as my opportunity to give back to the many threads in my tapestry by sharing the lessons I had gleaned from them.

Right when you think your tapestry is complete, when every inch of it is covered with threads, you will realize all the extra trimmings, the fringes and the tassels you have yet to add. And, as with your tapestry, you will find all sorts of elements can be used for your trimmings, from the most luxurious silk to the roughest rope. The only thing to keep in mind is that many trimmings, such as tassels and fringes, are free-moving extensions that should be constructed with movement in mind. They should be able to move freely without worry of becoming tangled or dislodged. These trimmings are your opportunity to enhance the threads in your tapestry. When you choose to draw out certain threads for use in your trimmings, you not only spotlight the important elements that are your essential makeup, allowing them to highlight the variety of colors in your tapestry, but you offer others something to latch onto if they so choose.

THE HEARTBEAT

HAVING ROUND, WIDE EYES, and a fine china complexion, the endearing term "doll face" is a perfect fit for the lady who inspired Frank Massi, former president of the Hearst Corporation. She was the modern heart of our massive media company—a "family" lady who always focused on us as members of her own special family.

Most corporations tick along with a metric of budgets, plans, strategies, and decisions on growth, acquisitions, personal staffing, and financial performance. Our Hearst was no different in all the years I had contact with their senior management. It was an efficient, premier media company with a century plus heritage and reputation as a product/talent driven place. What it did not have was the gentility of atmosphere at the corporate level that would give one the sense of always being in caring hands.

Madeline Massi was only herself as she saw her Frank ascend to the presidency of the place. That self recognized the names of his colleagues and their spouses, and the names and special circumstances of each couple's children had she met them—even if only once. Her face, her smile, and the tone in her voice all saluted everyone she met and gave each a sense of value and of being appreciated.

The Massis' summer vacations always included a trip to Saratoga Springs, New York, just outside of Albany, where I was privileged to be publisher of the Hearst newspaper, the Albany *Times Union*. It was our special pleasure when Frank and Madeline Massi would stop at our home for a personal visit on their way to Saratoga. During each such visit, Madeline always asked that each of our children come warm her lap. She was bouncing our second daughter, Marsha, on her experienced lap when Marsha looked out the front window and noticed the large black limousine waiting for the Massis. Marsha, who was then undergoing radiation for bone cancer, has always been attracted to the elegant. When she saw the limousine that day, she said she dreamed one day she would ride in such a car.

The next day we received a call from the limo driver, who inquired at what time he might pick Marsha up and bring her to a private lunch in Saratoga with Mrs. Massi. We set the mid-morning schedule and off went our tiny doll of a daughter seatbelted into the middle of the massive black velour seat, as she set off for a one-on-one tea with the wife of the company president. Marsha was returned later that day with Madeline accompanying her. She thanked us for the privilege of sharing our daughter.

Madeline infused that same largeness of heart into everyone she touched. Sadly, while Frank Massi passed away, what will never pass is the lingering goodwill of one lady choosing to share the abundance of her heart with us all. She became a thread in so many tapestries that in turn reached out with a fresh heart to other colleagues to extend the cherubic way of such an angelic soul.

In sharing my plans to study angels, I not only opened myself to receiving stories from the tapestries of my friends' and colleagues' lives, but also to almost every chain e-mail letter dealing with kindness and angels. The following anonymously written story is one of them:

His name was Fleming, and he was a poor Scottish farmer. One day, while trying to make a living for his family, he heard a cry for help coming from a boy. He dropped his tools and ran to the boy. There, mired to his waist in mud, was the terrified boy, screaming and struggling to free himself. Farmer Fleming saved the lad from what could have been a slow and terrifying death.

The next day, a fancy carriage pulled up to the Scotsman's sparse surroundings. An elegantly dressed nobleman stepped out and introduced himself as the father of the boy Farmer Fleming had saved.

"I want to repay you," said the noble man. "You saved my son's life." "No, I can't accept payment for what I did," the Scottish farmer replied, waving off the offer.

At that moment, the farmer's own son came to the door of the family hovel. "Is that your son?" the nobleman asked. "Yes," the farmer replied proudly.

"I'll make you a deal," said the nobleman. "Let me take him and give him a good education. If the lad is anything like his father, he'll grow to be a man you can be proud of."

In time, Farmer Fleming's son graduated from St. Mary's Hospital Medical School in London and went on to become known throughout the world as the noted Sir Alexander Fleming, the discoverer of Penicillin.

Years later, the nobleman's son was stricken with pneumonia. What saved him? Penicillin. The name of the nobleman? Lord Randolph Churchill. His son's name? Sir Winston Churchill.

I was so intrigued by whether this story was true or not that I did a little bit of research after receiving the email. Although I found a few discrepancies as to the consequences surrounding the saving of the nobleman's son, the one common thread I found was that, because the nobleman's son was saved, and he repaid this kindness by sending the farmer's son to school, not only was the life of the nobleman's own son saved again, but also the lives of millions around the world. Isn't it amazing what a little kindness can accomplish?

DO THE RIGHT THING
BY TRICIA BUHR

I NEVER REALLY THOUGHT about it. I am a positive person. It is not something I consciously strive to be; it is what comes naturally to me. Although my positive outlook has been the source of my happiness, I never wondered how I got that way—until I was asked to write about threads of angels who had a positive influence on my life.

At first I thought, *Let me share one profound moment.* What about that homeless man who swaggered past me as I crossed a stone pedestrian bridge over the Charles River one crisp Boston morning? "It's the trip, man. It's not the destination. It's the trip. That's what's important."

Wow, that could be my mantra. I remember looking into a mirror as a teenager one day and recognizing that, no matter where I was or what my profession turned out to be, my calling was to build a good place and foster a joyful journey for the people around me, to travel with others in this life meaningfully and gracefully. "It's the trip, man. Not the destination."

Then I recognized the most profoundly angelic influence of all. God blessed me with an angel who taught me to be good and to be open to goodness, weaving the most beautiful parts of the tapestry of my life. And, I have been calling her Mom.

"Do the right thing and you will be rewarded. It may not be right away, but if you do the right thing you will be rewarded."

Looking back now, I realize her positive message was more than a well-fashioned platitude, and it was more than that message that guided me. Mom lived it, doing the right thing naturally and joyfully. After my father passed away at all too young an age, Mom raised six kids all by herself. She worked full-time at the phone company and came home every night with enough energy to cook, clean, run the household, meet with teachers, and encourage and love us, all with humor and grace. She never complained about cosmic injustices and never gossiped about co-workers or neighbors. And above all, she always found the best in people. She invited children, lonely neighbors, and relatives into her home, and cared for them when their families could not. One late night she even pulled a nearly passed out drunken stranger from his car and into her kitchen, serving him coffee until he was in better condition. Mom has an unshakeable credo that doing the right thing is the right thing to do.

Now, when she plays with my own child, I witness the sharing of her beauty and am moved to tears by this angel. Today, as she shared a laugh with my toddler son, she leaned over and said to him, "Life is fun. You are going to have a wonderful life."

This gray-haired mother and grandmother is a true angel thread in my life. She wove into me a faith that doing the right thing is the right thing, and she is weaving into my small son the same joy of living. May she be rewarded one-hundred-fold.

"Life begets life. Energy creates energy.
It is by spending oneself that one becomes rich."
—SARAH BERNHARDT

HAVING NOTICED SOMEONE is in need of help, do you stop
to see what you can do, or do you keep moving on your way?
We are often presented with opportunities to help others,
without a clear plan detailing what the effects of doing so
will be. And, as was the story with Sir Alexander Fleming
and Sir Winston Churchill, sometimes what we consider a
small kindness can make a difference to the entire world.

My Babysitter

NOW, WITH THE DOOR open to explore the magic of the
speaker's platform, I began to volunteer to speak at colleges and universities whenever I could tie such events into
my regular business trips. In fact, since I was appearing at
several journalism schools, that fraternity of professionals
began to suggest to counterparts around the country that
I be invited to speak.

With invitations now flowing, as I mentioned earlier,
my blind teacher pal Rich Ruffalo introduced me to Nancy
Vogl over the phone. Nancy had been gracious but firm
in telling me she only agreed to handle and represent a
speaker after she saw him or her in person. She asked me
to let her know of any upcoming speaking event. Some
months lapsed before I received an invitation to speak to
several classes at the University of Georgia. Alerted, Nancy
changed her plans and agreed to come and hear me.

We were guests of the University and were both accommodated at a charming downtown Athens bed and breakfast. The informality of the B & B invited a relaxed discussion over both breakfast and dinner.

Nancy explained that if she agreed to handle me as a new speaker, she would only do so if I agreed to permit her to develop all my marketing materials and also abide by her critiques to improve my delivery. I agreed. She did attend each of the lectures and over lunch paid me the great compliment of telling me I reminded her of her favorite speaker, the recently deceased Og Mandino. I, of course, had spent hours listening to tapes of Og, courtesy of Dr. Rob Gilbert.

Very quickly, I learned just how serious Nancy was when she had dictated those terms to me. She became a whirlwind of competent guidance in the development of speaker kits and video samplers to send prospective clients. Every word of every piece was edited and approved by Nancy Vogl. I called her my "babysitter."

In the process, I came to learn how this remarkably finished professional bureau owner had left a brutal marriage, while expecting her third baby, with no college education, no true skills, no craft. Married right after high school and quickly becoming a full-time mom, Nancy had never had the opportunity to reach her full potential. Moving into a small townhouse without transportation, sporadic child support and many challenges, Nancy resolved she would one day achieve self-independence. Armed only with her grit and determination, she was inspired to bring first-rate speakers to her hometown, East Lansing, for major civic events.

Indeed, having by now worked at a collection of jobs, she had a sense of her own organizing abilities and had purchased a car. Using it as collateral, she persuaded a local bank to advance her the funds to lease the local performing arts center at Michigan State University and reserve some specific dates for several world class speaking events.

She announced that she would present the renowned author, Wayne Dyer, as her first speaker. The only flaw in her plan was that she had not yet been able to get Dr. Dyer to agree to speak at the inaugural event. With her phone calls and letters all ignored, and the calendar ticking away, Nancy made one final attempt via an overnight letter to Dr. Dyer's summer home in Hawaii. Nancy's nervous communications had been filled with great emotional pleas. It suddenly struck her that she had not approached Dr. Dyer from a business viewpoint. Only six weeks away from her scheduled event, she decided to lay out her entire business plan for this event from the marketing to ticket prices to explaining her mission. However, at the end of this lengthy report, she couldn't resist one small, impassioned statement. She wrote, "Dr. Dyer, I just read your new book, *You'll See It When You Believe It,* and I believe with my whole heart and soul that I'm meant to bring you to East Lansing, Michigan. You can't say no!"

Possibly struck by her daring tenacity, needless to say, Dr. Dyer said "yes" and her first event sold out the 2500-seat auditorium! Nancy went on to bring in other illustrious speakers including her favorite event featuring Dr. Norman Vincent Peale on his 93rd birthday and famed author, Og Mandino. The impressive sold-out event, which turned into a spectacular birthday celebration for Dr. Peale, was a testament to Nancy Vogl's determination, wonderful organizing skills and "never give up attitude." From these successful events, Universal Speakers Bureau evolved.

Petite, bouncy, full of robust enthusiasm for the speaking profession, Nancy signs all her correspondence with a heart bursting with love. She brings that heart to everyone she serves. It pulses most vibrantly when those of us privileged to be in her speaker family see her as a devoted mother to her lovely three daughters and her handsome grandson, Tyler. Nancy Vogl had been a vital thread in my speaker tapestry. She still is my babysitter.

BEING A "BABYSITTER" is often what the trimmings part of our life is about. Although others are usually quite capable of taking care of themselves, sometimes a simple act of kindness can make a world of difference.

I found one such example in the following excerpt of an article from *Ladies' Home Journal*:

Roma Downey, who stars as the angel-in-training in the TV phenomenon "Touched by an Angel," is the first to admit that she's not always up to the role offscreen. Cozily curled up on the couch in her Salt Lake City home, she shares a story that haunts her to this day.

The thirty-three-year-old actress was boarding a plane from New York to London a few years ago when she came upon an old woman struggling up a ramp. "She looked lost and quite terrified," explains Downey with her cheerful Irish lilt. "I asked if I could help her, but she didn't speak any English." With gestures and smiles, Downey convinced the woman to accept her help to the back of the plane. When the flight was over, the actress, who was seated up front, was anxious to disembark and catch her connecting flight to Dublin. Then she remembered the old woman. "'A flight attendant will surely help her,' I told myself. 'But if you get off the plane, you're rotten.'"

As she recalls she didn't really want to wait, but a small voice convinced her to stay put, and sure enough, the passengers getting off the plane did not include the old woman. "I went back, and there she was, waiting," says Downey, who arranged for a wheelchair and stayed with her. "And now I'm thinking, I'll have to take this woman home with me! Finally a young man, whom I'm guessing is her son, comes, and there is a warm embrace."

Relieved of her duty, Downey went to collect her luggage. Suddenly, the young man was beside her, tugging on her arm. He said, 'She wants me to translate. She is saying, "I prayed to God to help me on the plane. You must be an angel."'

THOUGHTFULNESS IS CONTAGIOUS
BY NORA ANN HUGHES

YEARS AGO MY HUSBAND went through an experience that would change both of our lives in many ways. Laurel Brown, whom we had just met six weeks before, added a special touch to a stressful time.

Let me back up and fill you in a little. Mutual friends invited us to a New Year's Eve dinner party at the home of Laurel & Joe Brown. Being new to our community and with no special plans for New Year's, our friends thought we might enjoy meeting the Browns and a few other couples. Needless to say, we had a wonderful time. Laurel and Joe were extremely gracious and welcomed us warmly into their home.

Six weeks after meeting the Browns, my husband went for a stress test, which was scheduled after he occasionally had shortness of breath. Much to our surprise, he wound up in the hospital immediately after the test. A catharization was performed and, because his arteries were almost completely blocked, he was scheduled for quadruple bypass surgery at 7 am the following morning. Five days after the surgery, he was home from the hospital. So, with no damage to his heart, his recovery progressed nicely.

This is when Laurel became a special person to my husband and me. While he was in the hospital, she called several times inquiring about progress and offering to help me in any way she could. Remember, we only met Laurel once just six weeks before the surgery. While he was recuperating, he began receiving cards from Laurel. They arrived at least once a week, each time with a little note to cheer him up. She kept the cards coming the entire time he was home. This meant so much to the two of us, but especially to him.

Because of Laurel's thoughtfulness, we have also followed her example. We have had several opportunities to send cards to friends and family for various illnesses. We keep the cards coming as long as necessary, just as Laurel did.

"Miracles… seem to me to rest not so much upon faces or voices or healing power coming suddenly near us from far off, but upon our perceptions being made finer, so that for a moment our eyes can see and our ears can hear what is there about us always."
—WILLA CATHER

I HAVE ALWAYS THOUGHT myself to be extremely perceptive and in tune with the world around me. I felt that my experiences had equipped me with a clear view of the world. I was wrong. Although my eyes had been open, it was not until the idea of *Angel Threads* came to me that I could really see.

Once I started researching angels and asking others to share their angel threads with me, I realized how limited my perception of what I thought I understood was. This happened for the most part, because I began to realize that there was so much more to life that I had yet to discover. Where I had once accepted coincidence without the hint of question, I inserted the joy of wonder. Instead of simply accepting the world, I began to question. Moreover, in doing this, I found myself back where I began, as a child coming full circle. Everything I began years ago seemed to come together. The purpose of each thread I had accepted into my tapestry, and how each thread seemed to give birth to another, finally became clear to me.

THE MORE IN "LESSNE"

DURING THE TIME I was writing my first book, *The Leader Within You*, I had been producing small laminated motivational cards to distribute at the college lectures I gave. After listening to one of the Og Mandino tapes provided by Dr. Rob Gilbert, I decided to use one of Og's profound quotes on one such card that I had labeled Vitamins for the Spirit. Research told me the quote I wished to use was from a book published by Lifetime Books of Hollywood, Florida.

Having already determined not to submit my new book to our own Hearst Corporation book companies, since I thought they might agree to publish as an act of friendship or charity, I was curious to know why the bestselling author Og Mandino would be published by a small Florida-based book publisher. I called and asked whether I might come by during my next visit to Florida. The publisher, Don Lessne, agreed to see me and we set a date to meet. However, he had cautioned me upon hearing a description of my book, that Lifetime did not have a high interest in a business-oriented work.

When we did sit down to meet, it was a cordial, productive meeting. He agreed to review my manuscript with a promise that he would give me an answer within two weeks. However, he cautioned me to understand this book might be outside their area of interest.

Just nine days later, Don called to tell me he had read the manuscript, liked it, and wanted to send me a contract and publish. What a thrill!

Don did not simply publish the book. He guided me in the necessary marketing, promotion, publicity and book signing tours to give energy to the sale process. In fact, when I began my book publicity and signings in Florida, I recall Don meeting me at 4:30 AM in order to have me at 6 AM Miami television show. The Lessne family all gave me more than was required. Don gave me more insights into the after-marketing work and Barbara, his wife, helped by assessing my interviews and suggesting comments to strengthen them.

As I put my fingers to the keyboard in registering this work, I did so with the fresh comfort of knowing so much more about the inside of the book publishing world. All threads vibrating in this portion of my tapestry weaving are called "author." And all those threads are interwoven as they flow from Dr. Rob Gilbert introducing me to Og Mandino's tapes; Rich Ruffalo opening the door to Nancy Vogl, she, herself, the great fan of Og; and my calling Don Lessne for permission to access a quote from the Og Mandino book he published. Og Mandino left indelible messages of hope and possibility in his books and tapes. He embraced a unique tapestry for the spirit of every person he touched. His books and speeches all beckoned readers and audiences to weave a life of achievement and serenity. Angelic Og.

Spiritual Oasis

HOPE IN THE BALANCE
BY SUSIE MANTELL,
STRESS-MANAGEMENT CONSULTANT AND AUTHOR

In July of 1991, in a tiny room in Arizona's Sonora Desert, my life, in fact my fundamental understanding of why it is we are here, was forever transformed.

I had come to this place from my home in suburban New York, pretty much "running on fumes." Anyone who has cared for a loved one slipping slowly into the abyss of life-threatening illness will understand the bone-weary grief and fear and exhaustion I had known for the previous eight months. (If you happen to have done this caregiving while teaching six-year-olds with special needs full-time, and working as a free-lance pop songwriter, then you will really understand.)

I believe we come here with purpose, and my joy and understanding of the intricacies of how we each develop, how we connect with that purpose and communicate, all provided ways in which I hoped I could reach and be of service to children and their families.

Six is a wondrous age! I thrilled to the expectancy and unbounded energy that ran and skipped, or cautiously inched into my classroom each September. I tied sneakers, counseled anxious parents, and guided their children into a world where we explored the mysteries of bubbles, earthworms and snow, and decoded phonetic symbols to give written language meaning. Little fingers curled around crayons creating purple castles and heart-shaped mountains on cards exclaiming, "I luv mi grama."

Each June, I would bid farewell as they moved on to new adventures and new victories. My summers were filled with adventures of my own graduate work, exotic travel and journeys into the wonder of Healing, in its many manifestations of body/mind/spirit.

However, in November of 1990, a family crisis called my attention and energy to a formidable and unprecedented challenge. My sister, Dale was evaluated at Yale for a heart/lung transplant. We were scared. Having lost my father to a brain tumor, I still struggled with regret over my helplessness as a child, as he had died slowly in the room beside mine. And now, another grave illness. Only this time, I knew about how to comfort. So, I drove those forty minutes after work to cheer, soothe, distract, shop for, mop and share tears.

Ours had been a complicated relationship, somewhat strained, but we were discovering an intimacy in this darkness, a tenderness we both cherished as we squeezed into those moments 38 years of questions, secrets and memories, getting to know one another. But she grew weaker. With all the love I knew, I would massage "what ifs" and "not yets" from her knotted muscles, gingerly avoiding surgical land mines and a torturous swath of Shingles.

Some days I would take her through guided imageries, and I wrote her a song called Lullaby, including a visualization of Dale, again healthy and strong. Our family listened to that song a lot. But when my own immune system crashed, I realized I was a completely run-down victim of "caregiver burn-out." My lessons tend to come hard, but they often bring along some remarkable gifts.

I have always "known" things about people, sensed energy with an innate understanding, a kind of compassionate sixth sense that guides me. And, something told me that I needed to restore my own mind/body/spirit in order to prepare myself for what was to come.

I flew to Tucson for respite and, thankfully, the Universe complied. I think I slept for the first three days, waking for the light meals and long walks on the warm desert earth, breathing air that had never seen the New York skyline.

One afternoon I told a woman I met of my desire to find a drumming circle, having heard about this powerful Native American ritual. Her eyes crinkled into a smile as she invited me to a small drumming scheduled that very evening at her house. (I love those moments! Synchronicity is, for me, a great comfort.)

The drumming was led by a local shaman, a woman in her early forties with the most extraordinary eyes I had ever seen—golden flecks in deep green pools that looked so deep inside my own it was a bit unnerving. She drummed and chanted, addressing the aches, pains, and woes of those present.

Still a bit skeptical, I described my own chronic shoulder pain. She began to "tone" a specific pitch that she hummed until I literally felt the vibration penetrate my scapula and the sensation of a stone dissolving into granules, the familiar pain dissipating and then, gone. She spoke of an unusual energy she sensed. "You know you're very angel-connected, don't you?" she asked. To my genuine surprise, I heard myself acknowledge that I did. I had just never discussed it—ever. Refocusing her energy, the shaman looked again into my eyes, singing a childlike, made-up song. It sounded a little silly, until the last four words: "This is your lullaby." Stunned, I asked later what made her choose "lullaby," but she explained that her readings occur in an altered state of consciousness. She never had memory of them. I left that night a little "altered" myself. Pain-free and very, very curious.

Over the next two weeks, I met with her often, attending drummings in her simple desert home, processing inner conflicts and physical symptoms into emotional insights in sessions I can only describe as magical. Unquestionably, the most dramatic transformative experience I had with the shaman occurred in a private session, in which she guided me gently into a mildly altered state. As we reviewed my life back to infancy in images, she asked if I would like to go further, back into the womb. I experienced that time quite naturally, as if it were the present. Then she asked if I would like to go further still, to the time before my spirit entered this body. At this, I opened my eyes, squinted at her light-hearted, "Whatever you choose is fine with me!" expression and decided to go for it. What ensued was to forever change my understanding of why we are here. Suddenly surrounded by a radiant light—familiar some-how—we spent that afternoon together opening doors to my soul that would take me forward and, to this day, guide my choices and decisions in all things. That afternoon, from somewhere deep within and somehow all around me, I was given my etheric name, "Alaeia." It came in song—a choir of angels—but in a breath-taking form and rhythm I could never have composed myself. Over time, I could not ignore a familiar "knowing" in my solar plexus. I understood that somehow my intuitive use of imagery in healing, the inner wisdom of the body, and a sense of spirit, were where my creative energy was being redirected.

I returned from my trip to Tucson with restored vitality, renewed hope and many new tools to replenish my sister and myself. I created my protective rituals to maintain my equilibrium and before each visit would "parcel off " one-third of my energy to leave outside the door to await my return—one third of my strength and courage and love. Fortified with two-thirds of all I had to give, I could open my heart and offer it freely. Massaging, and wishing and reminiscing, reading aloud stories about others' encounters with the Divine, watching funny videos, giving pedicures, little by little, we found laughter and hope in some very dark places. And, little by little Dale stopped getting sicker.

One evening, about two years into her illness, I went to a club in New York City to hear one of my songs perform-ed. I was told the show was sold-out and I was crushed. Suddenly, a maître d' appeared and led me to a little table with a "reserved" card. There had been a no-show. On the reservation card was one handed-lettered word: "Alaeia." I thanked the maître d' (and the angels). I still have that card. Such synchronicities are, as those who know me will attest, part of every day in my world. It is who I am—who we all are when we trust it. In fact, I believe that the more we notice and savor them, the more they occur.

After two years of progressive debilitation, knowing recovery was not likely for my sister, we began to notice that some hours, some days, were "less terrible." Then, there were "good days." Then, a miracle happened.

Fast-forward ten months. I was standing on West 57th Street, the embodiment of sheer bliss, for one of my songs was to be performed on the stage of Carnegie Hall's Weill Recital Hall. At the same time, I ached with the knowledge that one very special face would not be in the audience with me that night. Chatting with friends, I felt a tap on my shoulder and turned to see, aglow in the streetlight, that face I knew so well! Oxygen cannula in her nostrils, with a portable oxygen tank in one hand, and a glorious bouquet for me in the other, she beamed, on this, her 45th birthday, "If this is how I go then this is how I go, but I am not missing tonight!" I remember a lot of hugging and tears, and I'm sure my song sounded just fine, too, but there were greater events in progress that night at the end of year number three.

Five years have passed since that night on 57th Street, and eight since my sister's devastating diagnosis. I am thrilled to report that my favorite patient is living a wonderful life. Now, a reasonable person might ask: Was it my desert experiences that redirected the course of events?

The unwavering love of her husband, devoted family and friends? Was it excellent medical care, or abiding faith, or the emotional healing she and I shared? Strangers in prayer circles in faraway cities, or a rekindled determination to stick around? I believe it was all these things. There is an inexplicable synergy that is set in motion when the spirit is hopeful. We become accessible to possibilities, new belief systems, and to Something Greater in and around us all. When love, faith and others support our deep desire to be well, sometimes miracles happen.

I am in awe of the journey and the angels along the way who carry us across the ravines. Through these events and those that brought me to them, my own career path had been exquisitely redirected as well. I followed my heart into mind/body wellness, specializing in stress-management. I now create programs for Fortune 500 companies, distinguished hospitals and world-class spas, and have been awarded special recognition as the author of *Your Present: A Half-Hour of Peace.*

In doing all this, I have come to honor, at a deeper level, the authenticity of the gifts with which I have been entrusted, allowing me to share them as I believe we are all intended, to facilitate others in discovering their own answers and their unique gifts. To be sure, some of our presents come wrapped in very ugly paper, but if we unwrap with care – hopefully and patiently – we are likely to discover possibilities beyond our bravest dreams.

"The tapestry of life develops thread by thread."

Parting Threads

When I first sent out invitations asking friends, family and colleagues to share their angel threads, I tried to be realistic about the number of replies I would receive. I did not expect the response to be so overwhelming, nor did I expect such a variety of answers. I only wish I could have used them all in this book. The following few are special gems that especially touched my soul, and which I hope you will choose to adorn your own tapestry with.

TEAM ANGEL
BY CAROL CURREN

THE LAST COGNIZANT WORDS words my husband's dying grandmother spoke to me, and they were spoken with conviction, were that I was going to have another child. She erroneously believed that my husband, her much beloved grandson, wanted a third child and I refused to have it. The truth of the matter was, neither of us wanted another child. We were blessed and content with two healthy, beautiful boys.

About a month after his grandmother died, and five days after I gave away the dust collecting crib in our attic, I found out I was pregnant. Cory was due around the first of January. We thought he would be early, as both his bothers were, but Cory waited a bit—until Friday the 13th to be exact. That should have been the tip-off.

Life with Cory has always been an adventure. At 18 months of age, Cory "ran away" from home. He escaped from the house while we slept. He climbed from his crib, unlocked the front door and traveled about five blocks, crossing a busy road, before a woman found him and went door-to-door in search of his parents. By the time Cory was three years old, he had already broken three bones. By age four, he was expelled from nursery school. Although we had suspected it for a while, Cory was officially diagnosed with ADHD (Attention Deficit Hyperactivity Disorder) when he was in kindergarten.

One evening, when Cory was about six years old, we tucked him into bed after the usual nighttime rituals. About an hour later, my middle son Adam passed by Cory's bedroom. He does not recall why he decided to check on Cory. It is not something this 11-year-old normally did. But the guilty look on Cory's face prompted Adam to call me upstairs for a check.

Pulling down the blanket, I discovered a package of grape-flavored, chewable Benadryl tablets. It was one of those push-through, foil, blister packs, and eight of the 12 blisters were empty. Cory confessed to eating some of them, but was not sure just how many. I called his pediatrician and Poison Control and was reassured that eating eight tablets was close to, but not quite lethal. I was to keep a close eye on him. Going back into his room, I still felt very uneasy. I began shaking his blanket and out fell another blister pack. It was empty. Realizing that 20 Benadryl tablets would surely be lethal, I yanked him up to rush him to the hospital. That is when he opened his hand to show me the 12 pills he had not yet eaten. Adam's discovery had been just in time to save Cory's life; if he had eaten the 20 tablets without being discovered, he would have simply fallen asleep and would never have awoken.

Until that day, I was not a particularly spiritual person—not much of a "believer." Cory changed all that. I know now that Cory does not have a guardian angel watching over him; he has a team of them! I was blessed with this child, who managed to be conceived in spite of appropriate birth control methods, for reasons that I might never know. But I know the reasons are important. Maybe in a former life I needed to learn patience and understanding. I am learning that now. I am also learning that this difficult, defiant, disruptive little boy has a kind, loving and forgiving spirit. He is bright, beautiful, and filled with hope and promise. I am a believer now. I believe with God's help and *Team Angels*, Cory will grow up to be a good man, strong, healthy and the source of great pride for his parents. And, the source of my growth, as well.

ANGEL WINGS
BY CINDY BAUMAN

LUCKILY, I HAVE BEEN BLESSED to have many angels cross the path of my life over the past twenty-eight years. One special angel recently received her wings and will remain in my heart forever.

St. Mary's parish in Pompton Lakes is a very special place, and all of its 11,000 members know that it is unlike any other Catholic parish. In the fall of every year, the women of the parish host a retreat called Cornerstone. In 1996, I decided to attend since I was a new member of the church and wanted to meet other women. On the retreat, I met many wonderful, kind, and spiritual women who shared stories about their lives and how God helped them through turbulent times. We shared, laughed, cried, but most of all we bonded.

We formed such a special, warm and caring fellowship in the group that I always felt comfortable calling any one of them and discussing problems. One woman, Lucille Hoffman, was especially precious to all of us. Lucille was gifted in many ways. She was our resident artist and helped design different aspects of the retreat. She was always coming up with great ideas on how to make the spirituality come alive for the retreat participants. Last fall, I was paired with her to co-chair one of the largest committees—Ambiance. She helped me to spark an interest in my own creativity that I still carry with me today. And, when I had to have unexpected surgery, Lucille took on my responsibilities as well as calling me daily to see if I needed anything during my recovery. This was one example of how Lucille constantly put other people's needs before her own and had a way of making them feel so special and cared for every time.

About two months away from retreat, Lucille told me she had not been feeling very well. She went to her doctor and he did some tests on her. She was in and out of the doctor's office and had to go to the hospital for further testing. Finally, she found out she had ovarian cancer, one of the deadliest and swiftest moving cancers. Lucille did not want people to feel sorry for her or to make a fuss, so she did not tell many people about her illness at first. When she came to one of our large group meetings and we asked for prayers at the end, one of the women asked us to pray for Lucille. That was when Lucille finally told us what was going on.

Lucille was not able to finish planning the retreat since her illness progressed so quickly. I felt an empty hole in my heart as I moved through the motions of getting ready for Cornerstone. I did what I could to help cheer her up, sending cards and calling her occasionally. On retreat, we each wrote her a love letter that her daughter read to her in her room in the hospital after a bad chemotherapy treatment. We had a prayer room set up for the retreat, where women took turns praying for 24 hours straight. Although the primary purpose was for the retreaters, I knew the core group of women was also praying with all of their hearts for Lucille. Sadly, she passed away just five short months after her diagnosis.

Lucille's funeral service was the most moving ceremony I have ever experienced. While her daughter was giving the eulogy, sharing how much her mother meant and would be missed, the church bells unexpectedly began to toll. I was sitting with my fellow Cornerstone women in the back of the church. We looked at each other and smiling through our tears, began whispering to each other, "Every time a bell tolls, an angel gets her wings."

THE POWER OF LOVE
BY MARK MILLER

I WAS 22 AND HAD been dating, and was serious enough about my future wife to want her to meet my grandmother, a woman of wonderful patience, wit and humor. We spent many Saturdays together, as I would bicycle about two miles to her apartment and go out to lunch with her at the Tiffin shop in Garden City, Long Island. She would always ask the waitress to remove the crust from my traditional chicken sandwich and we would talk about what was going on in my life. This tradition started when I was twelve and went on for many years.

My grandmother was quite ill; I never knew how much she was suffering. This time I drove to her apartment for the first and last meeting she would have with the woman I loved. We knocked at the door and her sister answered and asked that we wait in the living room so that she could announce to my grandmother that we had arrived. Soon we entered her bedroom, with the warm and defined rays of sunbeams glowing on either side of her bed, reflecting in a strange way through her beautiful white hair almost causing a glow to match her smile. "Grandmother, I would like you to meet Linda, the girl I am in love with."

She responded with a wonderful smile and said, "Come here my child and sit by my side." She took Linda's hand and said that she was so glad to meet her and what a beautiful young girl she was. They talked and laughed together and as we left she said that she was so glad to see my Linda. "She had such a beautiful smile and such lovely dark hair."

I went home that day, some 30 years ago, feeling good that my grandmother had approved and felt that Linda was someone special for me. I told my mother the story of our day, and she said that she was glad that we had all met since my grandmother was quite ill and had become completely blind a few months ago. I will not forget that day since she seemed to see as if she had sight. Perhaps it was the power of love.

A CHARMED LIFE
BY TINSLEY & SUZANNE RUCKER

OUR FAMILY OFTEN JOKES about our youngest daughter's guardian angel being on duty twenty-five hours a day, every day, Monday through Sunday. We are convinced she leads a charmed life. How else could we explain her numerous triumphs over adversity not of her making? Why else would she continue to greet each new day with a smile?

Though Nicole appears outwardly to differ from many other people, her resilience, persistence, positive attitude and faith make her quite remarkable, considering the series of illnesses and other challenges she's overcome. Somehow, there has to be an invisible guiding hand nudging her to remain open to new experiences and people when she could easily become frustrated, embittered and angry.

The obstetrician delivering our almost lifeless Nicole told us the odds were against her surviving. If she survived, she would be severely mentally retarded because of the undetected premature rupture of her mother's placenta and subsequent early birth. Nicole was alive against the odds she faced. Somehow, she was meant to be a part of our lives—a gift from God with a special attendant to protect her when we could not.

With all the attention given her early arrival, no one realized Nicole was born with a malformed right hip socket. At fourteen months of age, Nicole was placed in a body cast extending from her chest to her right foot and to her left knee. She learned to crawl hand over fist dragging her cast bound body wherever she wanted to go. A special circular walker allowed her to use her left foot to propel herself around outside. At age two, she took her first unassisted steps and quickly learned to walk.

Nicole's early elementary school years revealed an intelligent child with a good memory for detail and no ability to organize anything. When asked to clean her room, Nicole would sit for hours wondering what to do first and do nothing. Her writing skills reflected her inability to logically sequence her thoughts. Testing showed her to be in a group of children thought to have something newly labeled "attention deficit disorder." Though medication worked well, her already thin body could not tolerate the resulting weight loss. She would need considerable tutoring, family encouragement, and personal dedication to overcome her own body chemistry.

Over the years, Nicole attended a learning center after school several days a week and in the summer. With one-on-one attention, she excelled. She never tested well on standardized tests and refused to be officially labeled "ADD" by her schools. She was kept out of honors classes until she approached her principle about being bored. Nicole convinced him to allow her to take an English advanced placement course. Upon completing high school, she was in the top fifteen in her class.

In her middle school years, Nicole developed a fungal scalp infection commonly known as "monks" cap. Her beautiful long, fine hair fell out on the crown of her head. It would take almost ten long years for it to regrow. The unrelenting teasing of her peers could have made her a bitter young lady.

Instead, something inside her taught her tolerance and understanding for others. In class, and during band and cross-country, Nicole would console others and be a source of strength.

Rowing became a passion in college until she sprained an ankle and later developed blood clots in one of her legs. Her injury revealed she had a rare blood clotting disorder that could be fatal in certain circumstances. Within a year, she completed rehabilitation, was off medicine and again back on her team. Again, she refused to give up and settle for what might be the end of her rowing career. Failure was not an option.

Throughout her life, Nicole had been accident-prone—numerous spills on bikes, falling out of trees, and frequently requiring stiches. There was always something happening to her. One day, while riding her bicycle and not paying attention, she rammed a knee into a rear light of a small parked BMW. The car needed $600 of repairs and Nicole had to have a few stiches.

But, this was no woe-is-me kid. She might be fighting an uphill battle, but she always had an ear-to-ear grin. Some might call it the luck of the Irish, for indeed her heritage includes a wee bit of the Irish.

Whenever we look at Nicole's portraits from kindergarten to university graduate, we see two blessed beings—Nicole and her Irish guardian angel. Who else would work so hard for twenty-five hours a day?

NEVER ALONE
BY DR. BENJAMIN CARSON

A FEW YEARS AGO, I was visiting the city of Chicago for a conference. I decided to take the train from the airport rather than taking a taxi as I usually do in order to save some money. I carefully checked the exit that was appropriate for me and got off the train at what appeared to be the corresponding point. To my great chagrin, I discovered I was in one of the worst sections of Chicago, walking down a very treacherous appearing street with my suit and briefcase. I felt like a chicken walking through a yard of hungry foxes. As my anxiety levels began to rise, I prayed to God for deliverance, at which time a taxicab drove up, stopped, and the driver ordered me to get in. He said that I had no business in a neighborhood like that, and he proceeded to deliver me to my original destination. I rejoiced as that cab sped through the streets and when I exited the cab at the hotel, I was so joyful that I turned around to thank the cab driver, but the cab was gone.

That experience had a profound effect on me as I realized that no matter what danger I was in, God was still always in control. As long as my Father owns the universe and has legions of angels as his agents, I have nothing to fear.

About the Author

BOB DANZIG spent his childhood shuffling from one foster home to another, never quite belonging. When he got his first job as an office boy at the Albany *Times Union,* the newspaper became his family. Encouraged by a caring boss, he spent three years in the Navy; went to college nights for five years; was awarded a Journalism fellowship to Stanford University; and nineteen years after walking in the door as an office boy, became Publisher of the *Times Union.* Seven years later, he was named President of all Hearst Newspapers nationwide. In the next two decades, he led the 6,000-employee/colleague company to a renaissance of talent, strategic purpose, and 100-fold profit growth, earning him industry-wide respect for his innovative marketing leadership.

Today, Bob is Dean of the Hearst Management Institute; an inspirational author; and a spellbinding professional speaker, named to the Speakers Hall of Fame in 2007. He was the first recipient of the National Speakers Association's *"Philanthropist of The Year"* award; the first recipient of the Child Welfare League's *"Champion for Children"* award; and received the *2012 Beacon of Ethics Award* from the Business Ethics Alliance ®.

For Bob, the key to all these life marks is embracing every opportunity and acknowledging each individual who crosses his path. By spreading encouragement, enhanced spirit and confidence, Bob Danzig is bringing lasting change to a world searching for these qualities.

Books & eBooks by Bob Danzig

Conversations with Bobby
From Foster Child to Corporate Executive

Every Child Deserves A Champion
Including the Child Within You

The Leader Within You
Master Nine Powers to Be the
Leader You Always Wanted to Be

Angel Threads
Inspirational Stories of How Angels
Weave the Tapestry of Our Lives

Vitamins for the Spirit
A Collection of Insights to Enrich Your Every Day

Shakespeare Lives on Cape Cod (And Everywhere Else!)
A Tale of Comfort–Caring–Human Nature

Business Gems
The Softer Values of Success

You Are Full of Promise
Life Lessons for Leaders

www.BobDanzig.com

CPSIA information can be obtained at www.ICGtesting.com
Printed in the USA
BVOW08s0210020715

407186BV00001B/34/P